THE
RESCUE

THE RESCUE

OCTOBER 7 THROUGH THE EYES OF ISRAEL'S PARA-RESCUE COMMANDOS

GUY M.*

EDITING —JOE GAMSE AND JACOB ZUCKER

WICKED SON

A WICKED SON BOOK
An Imprint of Post Hill Press
ISBN: 979-8-88845-894-5
ISBN (eBook): 979-8-88845-895-2

The Rescue:
October 7 through the Eyes of Israel's Para-Rescue Commandos
© 2025 by Guy M.
All Rights Reserved

Cover Design by Jim Villaflores
Cover Photo by Amit Agronov-IAF

Orientation Map by Iftach Mashal

WICKED SON

Post Hill Press
New York • Nashville
wickedsonbooks.com
posthillpress.com

Published in the United States of America
1 2 3 4 5 6 7 8 9 10

The events, locations, and people in this book are all true places and real people from the terrible events of October 2023—people who were there on that devastating day and revealed their stories for the first time. Because Unit 669 members' identities must be concealed by Israeli army regulations due to the nature of the missions of special forces units, and the content is sensitive—and in accordance with the wishes of the protagonists—names, locations, and identifying features have been changed to protect their privacy.

*This book is dedicated to our friends
who have fallen so that others may live.*

With special thanks to Morris, Steven, Eli
StandWithUs, and the American Friends of Unit 669

TABLE OF CONTENTS

FOREWORD

October 7th, 2023
Morning

It had been less than two hours since I was thrown out of bed by the unexpected sound of the missile siren. It was a Saturday morning—the Jewish holiday of Simchat Torah—and Israel was under attack by the Hamas terrorist army in the Gaza Strip. Nobody had any idea what was happening. The banner on my TV screen still read: "PALESTINIAN REPORT: SOLDIERS ABDUCTED INTO GAZA." Nobody understood the magnitude of Hamas's invasion by air, land, and sea; the sheer scale of forces that had flooded into Israel; and the barbaric atrocities they were only just starting to commit in the kibbutzim[1] and at the Nova music festival.

Nobody. Not even Guy M.—one of the heroes of this war and the author of this book.

Guy and I had first met a few months earlier at a bar in Rabin Square in Tel Aviv, where we discussed the option of translating *Full Throttle: On the Edge With Israel's Elite*

---

1   *Kibbutz* (plural: *kibbutzim*): a small rural town in Israel that functions, to some extent, as a collective. Fully socialist *kibbutzim* were the backbone of the early Zionists' settlements, and the young state of Israel. Over the years, many of them privatized to some extent, but they all remain close-knit communities.

Combat Rescue Unit, a riveting memoir of his derring-do adventures as a pararescue soldier in the Elite Rescue Unit 669, which became a renowned bestseller. This was a chapter of his life he thought was behind him.

But since Guy had faced down terrorists before, I reckoned he might know something now. I texted him.

> *Have you been called up for reserves?*
>
> *Hey.*
>
> *Not yet.*
>
> *But Noga's already at the base.*
>
> *I'm focusing on my dad.*

Of course, his dad. Spoiler alert: Mr. M. had just had a major health scare on a family vacation, and as thousands of Hamas terrorists streamed into Israel, Guy thought he would stay to be with his dad at the hospital.

Look after yourselves, I texted Guy back. *What a nightmare.*

Absolutely, he texted back. *I think we haven't realized the magnitude of the event yet.*

Boy, was he right.

Four days later, I checked in on Guy again:

> *How's your dad? Called up yet?*

No response.

The next day, a voice note came through:

> *Hey man. We were among the first to reach the scene on Saturday morning. Atrocities the devil himself couldn't create. There were bodies every-where, and the kibbutzim were islands of ruins. We have started preparing for the next stage.*

That "next stage" came with writing a whole new book, one which Guy somehow wrote in between rescue operations of casualties from the battlefield, and top-secret missions throughout the war—and which I somehow translated in between a blitz of media interviews, as I found myself enlisted as a government spokesman on international TV.

I next saw Guy at his wedding with Noga, his irrepressible better half. Nearly all of unit 669, the whole cast of *Full Throttle*, was there on a short break from duty to celebrate with Noga and Guy. (When Guy describes each teammate in *Full Throttle* as a mountain of a man, he really isn't kidding, and they brag that as reservists, they are way past peak fitness.) Barely two weeks later, Israel awoke to the exhilarating news that two hostages had been rescued in a daring mission. I texted Guy again.

Were you there?

No, he replied. *But the guys you downed shots with at the wedding were.*

When the media reports on Israeli soldiers—about their military operations or tragic deaths—it is easy to imagine a breed of action men born for the role. There are civilians and there are soldiers. They are different species. But as we are reminded in *The Rescue* and *Full Throttle*, they are the same people. The same flesh and blood. In so many cases, civilians and soldiers in Israel are not different people; they are just different stages of life. And by "stages," I mean days, swapping over with dizzying speed. Fighting in Gaza one day. Downing shots at a wedding the next. And rescuing hostages from the depths of Rafah one day after that. They are trying to complete med school, to plan a vacation, to organize a wedding—and constantly on call to get called into action to defend family and friends from barbarism. Flitting between fighting and living the moments that remind you of what you're fighting for.

I hope you enjoy reading this book. It is a labor of love by author and translator alike. Let me take the opportunity in this foreword to apologize to readers that the events of the October 7 War dragged out the translation process for an unreasonably long time, depriving you of the adrenaline rush of reading about unit 669 astonishing operations and Guy's heroic journeys. I can barely believe they happened and looking back, neither can Guy. But they did.

This is our reality.

Eylon Levy
Former Israeli Government Spokesman
Translator of *The Rescue: October 7 through the Eyes of Israeli Pararescue Commandos* and the upcoming *Full Throttle: On the Edge with Israel's Elite Rescue Unit*

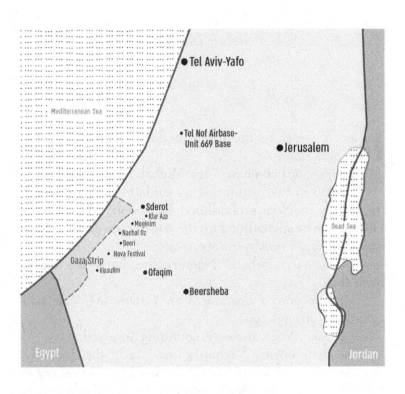

Tel Aviv-Yafo

Mediterranean Sea

Tel Nof Airbase-
Unit 669 Base

Jerusalem

Sderot
Kfar Aza
Meginim
Nachal Oz
Beeri
Nova Festival
Gaza Strip
Kissufim
Ofaqim

Dead Sea

Beersheba

Egypt

Jordan

PROLOGUE

October 7th, 2023
07:00
Guy

I open my eyes to the sound of loud knocking on the bedroom door.

"Noga, can I come in?" It's Michal, Noga's mother.

I sit up in bed, squinting as sunlight floods through the blinds in Noga's childhood bedroom. The house is located in a neighborhood on the edge of Jerusalem. *Since when does Noga's mom ever wake us up?*

"Mom, we're in bed," Noga replies, her voice hoarse from sleep.

"I know you're sleeping. Can I come in?" she asks again, in a strange tone.

"I guess," Noga answers, sounding annoyed.

The door opens. Michal is standing in the doorway. She clears her throat, her hands on her hips. "I'm sorry to disturb you, but the whole country is under missile attack. There are terrorists attacking places in the south. I thought to myself you might want to get up," she says in a high-pitched tone, somewhere between startled and sarcastic.

Noga leaps out of bed. "Shit, shit," she mutters, looking for her phone and seeing a flood of missed calls from officers in her battalion. Within two minutes, she's already in army fatigues, shoving extra shirts into a backpack.

"Guy, I'm off. Your brother called. He wants to get a ride with me to the base. I'll call you!" she shouts on her way out. The Beit Lid Military Base is home to the Paratroopers Brigade, where Noga does her reserve duty, and the Nahal Brigade, where my little brother Ari finished his military service just a couple of months ago.

I'm still in bed. I glance at my phone: "REPORTS OF A SECURITY INCIDENT IN THE SOUTH. ROCKET FIRE FROM THE GAZA STRIP. GAZA ENVELOPE RESIDENTS SHOULD REMAIN IN THE SAFE ROOMS."[2] I check WhatsApp. There's a message in my reservists' group: *No change in the unit's readiness status. If needed, we'll be in touch.*

I feel a sense of relief. I guess it's no big deal. As far as I'm concerned, I'm happy to stay near Jerusalem, where my dad is still in the hospital.

I get out of bed, but sluggishly, still drowsy.

"They haven't called you?" asks Roni, Noga's dad, in a confused but hesitant tone. His eyes are glued to the TV; I can hear the newscaster's voice in the background.

"I guess not." I sweep my hand back through my hair, inadvertently giving myself a sort of morning mohawk. "To be honest, I'd rather not go. Maybe they'll leave me alone."

"Your generation doesn't quite get this, but they don't always ask you politely to go to reserve duty," says Roni, shooting me a charged look. "There are times when you don't have a choice."

His words resound in my ears, and I write out a message to my reserve duty commander. *If you need me, I'm in the country, I'm available.*

I'm about to send it when, like a prophecy being fulfilled, the phone rings. It's my unit's coordinator.

"Guy, how fast can you get to the unit?"

"I'm half an hour from base."

"Great. Get here in twenty."

---

2   The "Gaza Envelope" (Hebrew: *Otef Aza*) is how Israelis refer to the areas of Israel bordering the Gaza Strip.

TO BE HONEST,
I HADN'T PLANNED TO

June 21st, 2023
08:00
Guy
The Biblical Zoo parking lot, Jerusalem

We're in the parking lot, I text the aquarium manager. *You're early. Be there in five*, he replies.

I take a deep breath and sit down on the hood of the car. There are no cars in the parking lot. A cool breeze, typical of a Jerusalem morning, strokes my face. Green winter foliage is giving way to the yellow tapestries of summer. Behind the bars of the gate, the workers are trimming the bushes and mowing the lawns. A large sign above the entrance reads "Welcome to the Israel Aquarium." Ari, my younger brother, is sitting beside me on the car's hood, his arms folded.

"So, Guy, are you ready?" he asks with a sly, knowing smile.

I answer with a nonchalant shrug, as if my insides aren't burning with excitement already. I'd been dreaming about this morning for so long, and as the big day approached, the excitement had only grown. This was the big week. I progressively got more and more stressed.

Last night, I couldn't fall asleep—I tossed and turned in bed, gripped by the fear that at the crucial moment, I'd forget everything I had planned to say. Or that even if I somehow remembered the words, I'd be overcome by emotion, and wouldn't be able to get them out.

"Do you think she knows?" I ask, without looking up. I generally don't smoke, but I'd love a cigarette right now.

"I don't think so," Ari says, calming me.

Ari just finished up his extended army service, which ended up being pretty varied. In his last position, he was a deputy company commander. He started out in a combat medics course, took a detour through Navy commando training, and ended up in the Nahal Infantry Brigade. He was deployed in Jenin for months on end, leading complex counter-terrorism operations almost every night in a city that was the epicenter of terrorism in the West Bank.

For Ari, being under fire from terrorists had become routine. When I heard what he'd been up to last night, I was terrified. I know how much he represses the dangers that come along with his job. It only really intrudes into his consciousness when his soldiers are injured, or when his commander, Bar Pelach z"l,[3] was killed in a clash with terrorists. All of us had been counting down the days until his long-awaited release from the army. And all of us were concerned that in one of his dozens of conversations with his battalion commander—who was trying to convince him to stick around—Ari would crack, and agree to extend his army service.

We all breathed a sigh of relief when he snipped his army ID card in half. Now, he's moaning about studying for the psychometric tests (the Israeli version of the

---

3   Z"l stands for *zichrono livracha*, Hebrew for "May his/her memory be a blessing."

SATs). He might complain but he's also taking on this new adversary with gusto (as he's done with so many others). It's the only way he knows how. I'm pretty sure he'd prefer an exhausting night drill carrying a stretcher along the Israeli coastline, or even a night spent arresting terror suspects in Jenin, to a day of studying. His friends suggested that he go abroad, travel the world, do all the things that just-released soldiers are supposed to do. No chance. Ari wasn't interested in any of that. He was determined to vanquish the psychometric test at the first attempt. And despite all of that, I'd known that if I suggested joining me at the aquarium—and if I let him in on what was going on—he wouldn't hesitate for a moment.

Noga's sitting behind Ari and me in the car. Her eyes are firmly planted on her phone screen, her thumbs tapping away. Every so often, she snatches a glance at the watch on her wrist.

"Guy, what time did you say we'd be done here?" she asks, without looking up. "I told Almog I'd meet her in the hotel lobby at ten."

"The manager's about to get here to let us in. I don't think it will be a problem," I answer, without looking around, nervous that my face will give away the maelstrom of emotions churning in my gut.

"You made such a big deal of arriving on time," she impatiently replies.

Ari snickers to himself. "All the stuff you've done," he murmurs, "and the thing that makes her suspicious is how much of a big deal you made of being on time. Maybe that'll teach you to stop being late to things."

I roll my eyes. "Check out this guy! Forget the psychometric test, maybe you should go into couples' therapy."

Our voices are hushed, and the deserted parking lot quiet, but my heart is pounding like crazy. I've been dreaming of this day for months. And I'd never have gotten here without the stubbornness of my friend Ya'ara. Really, it was all thanks to her.

Noga and Ya'ara had grown up together in a small town in the Jerusalem hills. They had been close friends ever since kindergarten, and all the way through middle and high school. They speak every week — and they tell each other everything. When Ya'ara enlisted in the IDF, she was sent into the Army's paramedic course — an extended year-long training that is led by the Israeli Red Cross, called Magen David Adom (the red star of David). It certifies one to treat casualties on the field like a physician. After finishing my training for Unit 669 as a rescue solider, I was sent to the course. That was a while ago, but Ya'ara and I stayed in touch.

After finishing my service, I went traveling to Australia. One night, at a hostel in the surf town of Byron Bay, I got a message from Ya'ara.

Guy, question: do you like redheads?

I only found out later that Ya'ara sent that message while out to breakfast with Noga. A few days earlier, Noga had split up with her boyfriend, who she'd been with for a few years, and Ya'ara had met up with her to see how her girlfriend was doing post-breakup.

"What are you doing?? Don't message some guy! It's way too soon!" Noga had said, trying to grab Ya'ara's phone.

"Calm down, it's nothing to do with you. I'm just texting someone from the Army," Ya'ara giggled. She swiped her phone out of Noga's reach, almost knocking over her coffee from the café table onto the sidewalk of the street in central Jerusalem.

"I literally just got out of the Army. I'm going traveling to Central America. Who knows who I'll meet there?"

But Ya'ara wouldn't let it go. Almost a year later, Noga was back in Israel to start a law degree at The Hebrew University of Jerusalem.

"I know he's studying medicine in Tel Aviv, which means he's stuck there for at least six more years, but just give it a chance. Trust me." Ya'ara kept pestering Noga, who was insanely busy, not only with her demanding university studies, but also with a stack of volunteering work and several initiatives to do with legislation and the rule of law.

Eventually, Noga carved out a free hour between meetings in south Tel Aviv, and agreed to meet Ya'ara's paramedic friend—mainly so that her friend would stop bugging her once and for all.

Our first date was at a bar in the Shuk Ha'Carmel market in Tel Aviv. It was a winter evening, and the rain was crashing down onto the tin roof above us. I'd come straight from the Department of Medicine's library, where I'd spent hours struggling with chemistry homework—a struggle that had ended with me slamming my laptop shut in frustration. My memory is that I'd been running slightly behind schedule. According to Noga, I was over an hour late.

He might become a doctor, he might become the President for all I care, I'm not going out with someone who's late for a first date. I'm out of here, she messaged Ya'ara from under the space heater of the deserted bar, a half-drunk beer in her hand. *Classic Tel Aviv player. Maybe he was different in the army. But in this town they're all the same.*

Ya'ara urged her to give this chronic latecomer a chance. She'd been working on this scheme for a year, but if I'd been late by another five minutes, all her efforts would have gone straight down the drain.

Drenched from my scooter ride through the rain, I sat down opposite the only girl in the bar. My own foul mood, the fault of those chemistry exercises, came up against an equally foul one across the table—a mood that seemed to be pointedly asking, "I came especially from Jerusalem for this date, and you're late?"

But within a few minutes, I was all in. It wasn't like she was trying to charm me—my lateness had made sure of that—but it didn't matter. She was nothing like any other woman I'd ever met. The sheer force of her personality lit up the entire bar. Her laugh and her beauty, both emanating from a freckled face and a mane of flaming copper-red hair, had me captivated. I suddenly had butterflies in my stomach. For the first time, there was someone I wanted to impress—someone whose heart I'd do anything to capture. And that was after only fifteen minutes together.

With the cost of living in Tel Aviv being what it was, I took a few different part-time jobs in the city, moonlighting alongside my studies. These included working as an occasional contributor to the daily supplement of *Yediot Aharonot*, a popular Hebrew-language newspaper. One day, I got a call from Elad, the deputy editor of the supplement.

"You hear about the Jerusalem Aquarium?"

"There's an aquarium in Jerusalem? What, like an underwater observatory? Never heard of it," I replied hesitantly, driving my banged-up car back from the university to the apartment I was sharing with two other students.

"They opened a marine life center with a huge aquarium at the Biblical Zoo in Jerusalem. Crazy project. I'm looking for someone to go diving with the sharks there and write up an article. You in?" Elad asked me nonchalantly, as if he didn't know that I'd bite his hand off at the offer.

At that moment, my thoughts turned to the redhead I'd met a few weeks ago—and the fact that I was supposed to be going out with her again that night. We'd already got to the point of speaking on the phone every day. The more our relationship developed, the more I was attracted to her. She was brilliant, full of energy, and with sky-high ambitions, but on any given day, she'd sooner go out partying with friends than study for her next university test.

I had a flash of inspiration. I called her—or, more accurately, I called the contact saved in my phone as *Noga Ya'ara Friend Date.*

"Hey, what's up?" Noga said when she answered.

"All good. How are you?" I replied politely.

"Doing well. We're on for later, right?"

"Yes, definitely. Random question—do you have a diving license?"

"Are you for real?" I could hear her smirking down the phone, as if I'd asked if she could read Hebrew. "I've done like sixty dives."

"So…how would you like to be the photographer for an article about the new aquarium at the Biblical Zoo? Some underwater photography in an aquarium full of sharks?"

FOUR YEARS LATER

Noga and I are living together in a small apartment in Tel Aviv. I'm starting my fourth year of medical school, and she's finishing up her law studies (on track to graduate with honors, obviously). She's already started working at one of the most prestigious law firms in the country. Soon, she'll start a year-long clerkship at the Israeli Supreme Court. We're running a household together; her friends are now my friends and vice versa. I feel like our relationship is in an amazing place. What's the rush to move forward to the next stage?

I grew up in a religious *yishuv*.[4] All of my childhood friends were already settled down with at least two kids. My friends from Unit 669, who've been with their partners since our army days, have started getting engaged. I understood it was time and I even knew how I wanted to propose. *But what's the hurry?* I thought to myself. *What are we rushing for?* I didn't think it was that important to Noga, either, that I proposed soon. Both of us were so busy with the craziness of life, and we were living together anyway. What was the point of having a big expensive party?

We went away for a short break, spending three days in Italy.

We were sitting next to each other on the plane, which had taxied to the end of the runway, waiting its turn to speed down the tarmac and soar into the air. Both of us were out of breath; we'd run the length of the terminal with the tightly packed carry-ons of a couple keen to avoid any extra baggage fees. We almost missed our flight—thanks to me, obviously.

I shut my eyes, intending to doze off, but Noga suddenly got out of her seat and turned to me.

"I can't take it anymore," she said, in a serious tone.

"Take what?" I replied, confused.

---

4   A *yishuv* is a small town or community in Israel. Unlike *kibbutzim*, they are not structured as collectives.

"I can't deal with the tension." She closed her eyes and took a deep breath, like she was about to blow up an over-sized balloon. "Are you going to propose?"

I froze for a few seconds, stunned by the question. I knew my answer would disappoint her, that it would be a huge letdown. I had no idea that she'd been ready and waiting for a while.

"To be honest—no," I murmured.

Noga didn't make a big deal out of it. But her disappointment made me want to find a unique, meaningful way to propose, something that would be such an amazing surprise, it would eclipse the disappointment she'd felt on that short plane ride to Italy. Easier said than done. Surprising someone as busy as Noga turned into such a convoluted operation that I began to think it was simply impossible.

A TOP-SECRET OPERATION

January 25th, 2023
10:00
Guy
Tel Aviv

Back in Israel, with Noga's expression of disappointment still hanging over me, I began planning the op. I was determined to surprise her with an amazing proposal—something she could never have dreamed of.

Step one: setting the date and time for execution.

I went over both of our calendars and found one free weekend—but only at the end of June. The silver lining of it being such a long way off was that it gave me plenty of time to plan the operation. I knew where I wanted to propose. The idea popped into my head one bright day, in a sudden flash of inspiration. I'd propose in the place where we'd really felt like we were together for the first time, holding hands down on the Jerusalem seabed, looking up at the manta rays and sharks crisscrossing their way through the water above us. I would propose at the aquarium, on the edge of the city that she loves so much.

I got in touch with the aquarium manager and he gave me the green light.

"It's a surprise. Please tell the workers and anyone else who might be there. I don't want us to get there and someone to say: 'Ah, you're the couple that's here to get engaged?'"

"Guy, you've told me a million times—it's a surprise. I get it. A. Surprise. You're coming to *research an article*," he'd answered, irritated. "Get here before eight in the morning, before visitors start arriving."

Straight after that conversation, I started looking up any flights abroad taking off from Tel Aviv late on that Wednesday morning. Straight after the proposal, I wanted us to head off on a romantic getaway. The flights that fit my time slot were to Cyprus or Johannesburg. Obviously, a proposal is a once-in-a-lifetime experience—but still, on a student's budget, there wasn't much of a choice. Cyprus, a mere forty-five-minute hop from Tel Aviv, it was.

"Noga, can you put in your calendar that we're going to the south the last weekend of June? Ron's throwing a party on the kibbutz, and he really wants us there," I off-handedly mentioned to her. The same night, as soon as she was asleep, I took her old iPhone out of the bedside table drawer and sent myself a list of her contacts—people in Noga's life whose help I'd really need to put the plan into action. Clearly, the first person I had to bring into the fold was Almog, Noga's boss. I'd never actually met her, but from the way Noga described her—well, the way she waxed lyrical about her—I was sure she'd be glad to help. As it turned out, Almog wasn't just prepared to help. She became a co-conspirator, bringing the entire firm where she was doing her internship with her.

"So that she has no suspicions at all, I've asked Noga to meet with the branch head, who's my boss—he's in charge of the department that I manage," Almog explained to me, in what became a daily phone call between me and Noga's boss. "We've briefed her on a secret client that's coming to Israel to initiate a takeover of a huge local company.

I've given her background material for a marathon of meetings with this secret client in Jerusalem, and we've explained that she can't discuss the case at all with anyone in the office. Don't worry—she'll be in Jerusalem with a suitcase packed for a few nights away."

"Wow," I replied, unsure if I was speaking to a lawyer or a screenwriter. "How did she take it?"

"Well…we only set up the 'meeting' with the secret client this morning, but she's already managed to ask me six times if I'm sure she doesn't need to prep for the meetings, or to get any legal background work done," Almog answered with a laugh. "But you know what a serious girl you're marrying. Are you surprised?"

To make sure Noga didn't suspect anything, I'd absent-mindedly let slip that I'd always wanted to visit Guatemala, and I suggested we go there for the Sukkot vacation in October. When I told her about the country famous for its volcanoes and why I wanted us to go there specifically, I dropped a few not-so-subtle hints that it would make the perfect place for some sort of romantic event. All the while, I was sorting out our Cyprus flights and hotels for the last weekend in June.

One day, with Noga by my side, I got a *surprise* phone call from the editor of the newspaper's weekend supplement, asking if I wanted to write an article on the new shark that had just been brought to the Jerusalem Aquarium. He suggested that I go scope out the place one morning—coincidentally, the very same morning that Noga was meeting her 'secret client.'

Noga, for her part, wouldn't tell me anything about the case or her client.

"I'll tell you all about it once it's in the newspaper," she said when I took an interest.

Ari was soon brought into the fold too. He was coming with us to "take a day off from preparing for the SAT test"—that is, to be our chauffeur to the airport. Noga's close friends were notified ahead of time so that they wouldn't try to make plans with her for the weekend of the operation; the supervisor of the course she teaches knew that she wouldn't be coming in that Thursday.

I even asked permission from Roni, Noga's father. She would get to the aquarium with a suitcase full of clothes for a frantic weekend of meetings, and a swimsuit so that she could dive with the sharks. Then, there was just one last thing—I couldn't forget to bring the ring I picked out with my mom. And our passports, obviously.

And then, the IDF decided to ruin my best-laid plans and started an operation in Jenin.

NOT THE TIME FOR JOKES

"Listen man, I told her to go home! I told her the unit's reserve duty is up. She's here by choice now," Ma'or, Noga's commander in the reserves, tells me.

Noga's last role during her regular service was as a company commander at the IDF's Officer Training Academy. After she finished her service, the commander of the Paratrooper Brigade asked her to become the Head of Operational Command for its Special Forces Battalion, called *Sayeret Tzanhanim*. As it turned out, she was the first woman ever to fill that role. I didn't love the fact that every few months she had weeks of reserve duty where they simulated warfare in Lebanon, in which she and the Battalion led paratroopers against squads of Hezbollah fighters. There were long weeks of drills where she'd been coordinating the combat operations of the regiments, defended only by a sheet of tarp tied to the Hummer that's somewhere in the mud of the Golan Heights. And now — it had to be this week — they've called her up to reserve duty again, as the Paratrooper Brigade is about to embark on an extended anti-terror operation in Jenin.

"I don't know what to do," says Almog, helplessly. "She says she's on reserve duty and can't get to the marathon of meetings with the secret client!"

I sigh heavily. "I just spoke to her commander," I say. Almog hears the despair in my voice.

"How about this," she says. "Let's wait another hour, and I'll try to speak to Noga again." She says it with the air of someone who's handled her fair share of crises. "Maybe I'll tell her we need her desperately in the secret client meetings. I'll guilt trip her for abandoning us."

It's late in the evening. In my conversations with Ma'or and Almog, I'm trying to figure out how to get Noga to the proposal as planned. At the same time, my two co-conspirators, Noga's commander and her boss, are helping me to not crack and just tell her the truth. Right before the proposal, after months of stress and preparation, I'd written out and deleted the words I wanted to say to her so many times. And right now, I'm dependent on the abilities of a senior partner of a huge law firm to convince a young intern that a huge transaction, worth billions of dollars, depends on *her* presence.

"Maybe it's worth having a backup plan," Ma'or says to me with a laugh. "It might not be such a bad idea to propose to her at the entrance to the base! You can bring some *shawarma* and *tehina*, that's a great way to celebrate."

"Too soon. I'm not ready for jokes yet," I reply coldly.

At the last possible moment, the stars somehow aligned, and Noga made it out.

"You're Guy?" asks the aquarium manager, deploying his apparently considerable acting skills.

"Yes—we spoke on the phone." I shake his hand. "Oh, and this is Noga and Ari," I add, gesturing toward the other two.

We follow him through the aquarium's entrance. Noga and I are holding hands; she's looking with an excited smile at the sea creatures of various types and colors on display through the aquarium glass. We walk slowly through the dark corridors that lead from one display room to the next in the giant complex.

"It feels like we were just here. I can't believe it's been four years already," she murmurs.

"Yeah, I know." My heart is pounding. I'm struggling to swallow. I draw my hand away from hers, in case she realizes how much I'm sweating from nerves.

We enter the central display room.

"I'll go behind the water tank and chuck in a few pieces of meat. That should bring the new shark to you guys—you'll be able to take some photos for the article," says the aquarium manager.

"I'll come too!" says Ari.

"What sort of shark is it?" asks Noga.

"I'll explain everything afterward," says the manager with a smile, and he and Ari disappear. They leave us alone, standing in silence under the azure glow of millions of liters of water, the shimmering outlines of the fish and sharks slowly gliding around us. The sounds of the sea emanate from the speakers all around the room. I'm struggling to hold it together. I feel like my legs are buckling under me. If I don't say something soon, if I don't finally let the secret that I've been carrying around for so long burst out into the space between the two of us, my chest will just explode. It's time.

Noga's gaze is fixed on the water tank, looking for the shark.

"Hey," I whisper, right by her, taking her two hands in mine. She turns to me, confused as to why I'm bothering her.

I pull in close to her, and murmur, "I'm the secret client, and the new shark—and I have a proposal."

TWELVE HOURS LATER

A sea breeze filters in through the open window. Stars glisten in the night sky. We're curled up together in the creaky bed at the hostel in Cyprus. A residual feeling of nervousness is still hanging around in my body. From the lobby, we hear the deafening sound of some drunk British tourists singing.

Both of us are the first children in our families. The first to do everything—and now the first to get engaged. Ari took us to the airport while we were calling and FaceTiming our families, and everyone's level of excitement was off the charts. The parents didn't know how to deal with this much happiness; they ended up going off to meet each other and celebrate together, without us. We kept up the virtual celebrations with everyone until we boarded the plane, but from then on, we were not in touch with them. We were only focused on each other, both awash with excitement and emotion, as if it were some sort of addictive gas we were inhaling from the air itself.

"I still can't believe it," Noga giggles, lying by my side.

"Me neither." I haven't even had the chance yet to explain how hard it was to plan the whole surprise operation.

Her eyes turn to the ring glinting in the dark. "It's so beautiful."

"You're so beautiful."

She rests her head on my body, in the little valley between my chest and my shoulder, like it's a pillow. Her skin, still wet from the shower, touches my chest, and the sensation sends a jolt of pleasure into my body, like the feeling of a gentle massage.

"You should know," she says in a whisper, turning her gaze from the ring to my eyes, "even today, after the best proposal I've ever heard of..." Her head is turned downward, her hair tickling my nose. "Even with all that—all the crazy stuff you organized—the best moment of the whole day is still right now. The moment that we're going to sleep at the end of the day, together."

THE HARDEST MOMENT
OF MY LIFE

September 30th, 2023
20:00
Guy
The Caucasus Mountains, Georgia
(South-Eastern Europe)

The croaking chorus of the frogs reverberates across the lake, and wisps of fog hover above its surface, disturbed only by the occasional ripples from the fish below. The horizon is punctuated with towering mountain peaks covered by evergreen forest, their dark shadows cast around the valley like a wall. We're taking a breather, sitting on the thin wooden jetty suspended over the lakefront.

"So Ari, you're flying to Nepal in a week. You excited?" asks Eden, my younger sister, the second-oldest of us four siblings.

"Yeah. I mean, duh, who wouldn't be excited?" he replies, with a typically macho, bro-ish energy, and stretches out in the chair.

"He meant to say, 'Yes, I'm really excited!'" chimes in Sivan, the youngest in the family, sardonic as ever.

Ari, who's sitting next to her, wraps his arm around her and pulls her tightly toward him, like he's trying to hug her into his chest.

"Stop Ari—you'll regret it. I'm stronger than you. I can beat you up and you know it!"

The two of them start grappling with each other. Eden watches, rolling her eyes.

"That's what I call brotherly love," I say. "This is exactly what Mom and Dad wanted us to come here for, right? To beat each other up?" I make my point and take a sip of the chilled Georgian beer in my hand.

Not long after Noga and I got engaged, Mom and Dad announced plans for what would be our last family vacation before my now fiancée became an official member of the clan. Itay, Eden's boyfriend of the last two years, wasn't far behind either. We used to laugh about how Noga and I were delaying Eden and Itay—that they were both desperate to get married, but were waiting patiently for me to propose to Noga first. It began as a joke, but Eden and Itai had stopped denying it. That was exactly what had been going on.

We hadn't been on a family vacation for almost a decade, either in Israel or abroad. There had always been at least one kid in the army, and my career-focused parents rarely took a break from work, so it was a big deal when they bought the tickets for all of us to go on a family holiday in Georgia over Sukkot. Ari was heading off on his long-awaited post-army trip a few days afterward.

That's how we came to be sitting at the edge of this small lake, next to our small hotel in some distant valley in the Caucasus Mountains. We're waiting for Mom and Dad, who are still getting ready in their room. Sivan and Ari have finished grappling, and Eden's taken up her role as photographer, directing them like models in a photoshoot. It's the absolute definition of a family vacation: quality time together, happy smiles all round.

I exhale deeply. I thank God for my good fortune. I'm having a great time abroad with my family. The photo-shoot that Eden's directing reminds me that Noga mentioned this amazing photographer she'd heard about, and that I'm about to marry the love of my life. We've set a date and chosen a venue at a kibbutz called Shefayim. More than anything, I'm reminded of how Noga's mom Michal, who has plenty of experience in event planning, fell in love with the place immediately when she saw that there was a hotel right next to the venue. In the middle of the night, when the party finishes, the entire family will be able to walk one hundred yards and crash straight into bed, and then, we'll be able to prolong the party atmosphere into the morning after. Invitations have gone out already, there's a photographer lined up, and a wedding dress is picked out. As it always is with Noga, everything's already organized.

"Guy looks pretty happy," I hear my dad's voice say. He and my mom appear out of the darkness, wandering over to us at their own pace along the pathway between the hotel rooms and the restaurant area. My attention snaps back to the present, but my mouth is still fixed in a contented smile.

"You guys ready to eat?" asks Dad. "I'm starving," he adds, not waiting for an answer.

"You're always hungry," says Mom, switching to English.

"*Nachon*," he says, switching back to Hebrew to confirm.

My mom, Betsy, grew up in Connecticut. After graduating college, she decided to take a gap year volunteering in

Israel. They sent her to this kibbutz in the north of Israel called Ramat Yohanan. Her mom (my grandma) wasn't so keen on the idea—and with good reason, because what she was concerned about was exactly what happened. She met a charming kibbutznik called Sagi, who had just finished his additional army service as a captain in the armored corps and was back for a year of working the fields. It was love at first sight. She worked next to him in the mango groves, lychee orchards, and avocado fields; they went for long runs through the hills all around the kibbutz; and he even took her on a few treks through the Sinai Desert. The second time they went to Sinai together, at the towering peak of the Bab El Donya mountain, with the Red Sea to the east and the Gulf of Suez to the west, and the horizon streaked with the burgundy of a desert sunset, my dad—without a diamond ring, not being burdened with American notions of propriety, but well-equipped with a clutch of dried dates and a jerry-can full of water—got down on one knee and asked her to marry him.

I was born four years later, on the kibbutz, like my father and his father before him. I was the fourth generation of family that were among the founders of both the kibbutz and the State of Israel itself. And yet, during my dad's undergraduate studies in Haifa, my mom managed to ignite his imagination, helped with his English and steered him through the unending bureaucracy and countless interviews that eventually landed him a place at Harvard for post-graduate Middle Eastern Studies. (These days, he's the president of the Harvard Club of Israel.)

When I was young, we spent almost four years in Boston. My mom worked at a Jewish nonprofit while my dad was studying, and at some point, Eden came onto the scene. Back in Israel, my parents started to become more engaged in Judaism and religion. My dad, who's proud of his kibbutznik background and isn't done with questioning, calls it "chasing after answers" (*lechazer achar hatshuva*) rather than "returning and repenting" (*lachzor bitshuva*) — and so we ended up moving to a religious town in the Lower Galilee.

As the children of sporty parents, we grew up in a regime of Spartan discipline. Karate, running, swimming, Pilates. Every day of the week, before the sun was up, you could find my mom riding her bike through the field after a brisk half-marathon-length run. After studying karate for many years, my dad founded a karate club in our community. All of us learned martial arts. When something good happens to any of us, we all know that someone will say, "It's all thanks to the karate." Over the past decade, my dad discovered meditation and Eastern wisdom; he began reading and studying more and more, and quickly started applying it to his daily life.

"Is there an English menu?" Ari asks a waitress with a striped apron, who's stationed at the entrance to the hotel restaurant. It's an unassuming Georgian restaurant, with dim lighting and crumbling walls. There are black-and-white photos on the wall, seemingly of families with many children, small packs of somber, unsmiling faces. The inviting smells of freshly baked bread and melted cheese fill the air, seeping into our nostrils and making us all salivate.

The portly waitress gestures toward a table in the corner. Mom and Dad sit on the same side of the table, still holding hands. My mom's face radiates happiness. She'd been looking forward to this trip for so long, looking forward to hanging out with her kids for longer than one day at a time. We come home on the weekends often, but typically, by an hour after Shabbat's over, we've all disappeared.

"There's like no veggie options here," says Eden, studying the menu like it's a math exercise.

"So, order a beer. That'll fill you up," I reply absent-mindedly, more focused on the restaurant's dozens of types of Khachapuri, a traditional Georgian plate.

"What's going on, Sagi?" my mom asks suddenly, looking at my dad with concern.

We all fall silent. In the restaurant's dim light, my dad's face looks off-white, like sour cream.

"I don't feel so great," he mumbles, wiping the sweat from his brow.

"Do you want to go back to the room and lie down?" my mom asks.

"I don't—"

His head plunges onto the table, his forehead crashing on his plate, cracking his glasses.

I'M ABOUT TO WAKE UP

September 30th, 2023
21:00
Guy
The Caucasus Mountains, Georgia

Ari leaps up from his seat, rounds the table, and lowers my dad to the ground, lifting his legs. I lean in next to him. His eyes are shut, his mouth open, and his face frozen. He's lying on the clammy floor tiles, unmoving. I place my fingers on his neck, gripped by a deep sense of dread. I keep my fingers where they are for a few seconds. Another second. And another. It's the worst possible situation. Get it together, Guy—there's no pulse.

"Ari, run, get the defibrillator!" I yell, and start CPR. Hunched over my dad's chest, I'm doing all I can to compress his heart and get some blood to flow to his brain. I know that I have to push harder. For chest compressions to be effective, you have to crush the patient's ribs, to feel the cartilage and bone buckling under your palms and hear them crack. I push harder, lifting and lowering my hips with every thrust, each one slamming my dad's head against the tiles. His face is motionless, his body limp. The restaurant has emptied out in an instant. No one rushes over to help—everyone's fled from the sight of me performing CPR. Ari runs to the hotel's front desk.

My mom and sisters are outside, standing on the pathway by the lakeside, screaming for help, trying to get someone who works at the hotel to call an ambulance. It's just me and my dad.

There's no way this place actually has a defibrillator, and there's no way to save someone that has gone code blue on the floor of a Georgian restaurant. *I can't believe this is where it ends*, I think to myself. I look at my dad's half-closed eyes. *You won't be with me under the chuppah,[5] which you were so looking forward to—you won't meet your grandchildren—we'll have to be there for Mom, there's no way she'll ever be with anyone else.* I keep pushing. Thoughts are racing through my mind. I think about how lucky I am that I don't have any regrets. *Everything I wanted to say to you, I said. Everything I wanted to do with you, we did together. Thank you for the amazing time together and for who you were for me.*

I say my goodbyes to my dad even as I'm thrusting down on his chest. His clean-shaven face looks calm—it's just my chest compressions that are disturbing his peace. It's like I'm annoying him in his sleep, a sleep that will last forever. I lift my head up, thinking to myself that I should try to preserve my last memory of him as alive and not a corpse. I look up at the dingy ceiling, praying for a miracle, praying that this is all a nightmare and I'm about to wake up.

Suddenly, I notice a movement in my dads eyes. This will be the toughest extraction of my life.

"Guy, there's an ambulance here!" my mom yells.

The medical team comes into the restaurant—two old women with a battered stretcher.

I rush them back into the ambulance, which turns out to be an estate car with space for a stretcher at the back.

---

5   The *chuppah* is the canopy at a Jewish wedding ceremony.

"Kislorod?" I snap at the elderly woman sitting next to me in the back of the car on the bench next to the stretcher, using the Russian word for oxygen. She shakes her head.

"ECG?"

She keeps shaking her head.

For God's sake, this "ambulance" has nothing beyond a red siren light on the roof and a few basic old bandages. They might as well have sent a mule-drawn cart. With the handful of Russian words I still remember from my paramedic training treating Russian-Israeli patients, I gather that we're twenty minutes from the nearest hospital.

My dad is barely conscious and can hardly respond to me. I give him an IV and try to boot up the old monitoring device bolted to the ambulance wall.

"Don't worry Dad, I'm here with you. We'll get you out of here," I say, over and over. I'm really talking to myself, grasping his flaccid arm with both hands.

After what feels like forever, we get to the entrance of the local hospital. My eyes widen in disbelief. A temporary streetlight, like the ones they put up when working on the highway at night, casts a feeble light over an elongated trailer park that leads to a darkened building. Some sort of grim Soviet fortress.

"Dad, we're here," I say, barely concealing my terror. I help the old women hoist the stretcher from the back of the battered old Volkswagen. He doesn't reply.

At first, they try to stop me from going into the emergency room with my dad. I explain that I am a paramedic who doesn't understand the language. The guard at the entrance gives up and lets me in. A few minutes pass; no one is paying us any attention. I fear for my dad's heart, suspecting that he'd suffered a heart attack and that, at any given moment, it might stop beating.

I take matters into my own hands. There's a saying in cardiology: *Time is muscle.* If my dad is really going through a heart attack, he would need cardiac catheterization as soon as possible. I take the ECG machine and start to check him out myself. I take a blood sample and make sure—with the help of Google Translate offline mode—that the worn-out nurse will send the blood off for the right tests. After a while, the nurse actually decides to assist me. I ask for drugs—aspirin and heparin—and most crucially, for the hospital Wi-Fi password.

With the help of frantic shouts in English rendered into polite Georgian by Google Translate and offers of payment in cash, a review of the correct medical procedures online with the attending doctor manages to convince her to wake the hospital's cardiologist. In the middle of the night, my dad undergoes cardiac catheterization, more CPR on the bathroom floor, a hurried transfer to a CT scanner on the other side of the building, and finally admittance to the hospital's ICU, which is less well-equipped than any family doctor's office back home.

Three ambulances and two sleepless nights later, we meet the rental plane that had brought an intensive care team in from Israel. Dad is lifted up on his stretcher into the front part of the tiny plane, next to the Israeli intensive care specialist and paramedic. Mom and I sit behind him. Before long, we're in the air. Even though he's now been transferred into the care of the best Israeli medical professionals, I can't take my eyes off him. My body is still tightly coiled, my ears zeroed in on my dad's heart monitor, as they have been for days, fearful of missing the telltale beeping that would signal another cardiac arrest. If I don't hear that sound, if I don't make sure he's being defibrillated immediately, he'll be dead because of me. In the seat next to me, my mom has a blanket draped over her head. The whole blanket is trembling, muffled sobs escaping from within it.

After a few hours, we make it to Ben Gurion Airport on the outskirts of Tel Aviv.

I didn't want to wake my dad up when we landed, so my clapping was much more muted than usual (it's an Israeli force of habit), but it was the most heartfelt round of applause I'd ever given for a landing. I'd never felt more relieved to see Ben Gurion's familiar control tower, and its airbridges snaking from the planes into the terminal building. Mom goes to pick up our car from the airport parking lot while I joined dad in the ambulance.

It is four in the morning. Here we are, speeding down Highway 1 in a United Hatzalah ambulance. I look out the window. I think about everything I've learned over the past fifteen years; all the skills and experience I've gained from volunteering at the local ambulance station as a teenager, from the combat medics course that all 669 rescue soldiers go through, and the additional year of paramedic training I was sent to by the unit after finishing the pipeline. From four years of medical studies. From my service in Unit 669, which trains you, among other things, to be assertive and creative. From working as a medevac paramedic for an insurance company, carrying out air extraction missions all over the world. It feels as though my entire life, without knowing it, I had been training and preparing for this moment.

Fifteen years that prepared me for the day that I'd be trying to save my dad's life, and to bring him home alive.

They've been waiting for us at the intensive cardiac care-department. Through the room's window, the early-morning sun casts a reddish glow onto the cream-colored houses of Beit HaKerem, a neighborhood adjacent to the Sha'arei Tzedek hospital in Jerusalem.

"Guy, go get some rest," my dad murmurs.

I don't even attempt to hide my exhaustion. I'm still straining my ears, listening for a sudden bleep from his heart monitor, as if my attention is the only thing preventing another cardiac arrest.

"You need to leave. It's not visiting hours now," says the nurse, firmly, steering me out of the room.

Noga's been waiting for me at the hospital entrance. She wraps her arms around me, and I bury my face in her neck. I close my eyes, and allow my body to unclench at last. *He's in the intensive cardiac care unit of a real hospital. He'll be okay*, I say to myself, not leaving Noga's embrace for minutes on end.

"We are so lucky that you were there at the right time," she whispers in my ear.

We head to her parents' place on the outskirts of Jerusalem and get into bed. I pass out in her arms before my head hits the pillow.

I stay in Jerusalem over the next few days, boomeranging between the hospital's cardiology department and Noga's parents' place. Roni and Michal take care of me with cooking and baked goods. "That's how we express love and compassion in my family," Noga had once explained to me.

Despite the maternal nurturing from Noga's folks, I'm not back to normal yet. I'm still exhausted and am having wild mood swings, which is exactly how I used to feel after crazy missions in the army. At night, I dream that I'm still in the 669 course, the grueling year and a half of training that makes a teenager into a special forces rescue operator who knows how to act when extracting casualties anywhere, anytime—whether by air, sea, or land. The last resort of any Israeli civilian or soldier. Eighteen months in which you can be kicked out at any point if you don't keep up with the team and team leader's pace. You're put under immense pressure and tested on a weekly basis through all the different trainings: commando warfare, Krav Maga, rappelling, parachuting, scuba diving, survival, and many more. Every time I fall asleep, I dream it's the middle of the night and I am scaling a mountain carrying a huge military rucksack. Even the initial try-out day for elite army units I went through when I was nineteen makes an appearance in one of my dreams. I'm crawling up a huge sand dune. Grimacing with effort, the sand fills my nostrils and eyes, with the screams of the different elite unit try-out instructors echoing in the background.

My mind, in its mysterious ways, is still trying to process what I'd just gone through. It's still trying to come to terms with the image of my dead father, with the creeping notion that I'd said goodbye to him forever. I try to file those memories and thoughts into the right section of my mental archive. The more serious the trauma, the longer it takes for the mind to healthily integrate the experience. My subconscious, meanwhile, connects the recent episode with my dad to the other traumatic experiences I've had, almost as if it's seeking out the ways I've managed to process them in the past. I'm almost thirty and, by now, I've learned that you must give these sorts of experiences time to fade; as they say, time heals all. But even so, there's still part of me that thinks that my dad died on the floor of that restaurant in the Caucasus Mountains.

On Friday night, we all gather at Sha'are Tzedek hospital. Mom's brought plastic containers full of food. We sit on plastic chairs around my dad's bed. As always, he blesses each of us in the traditional way. I bend down by his bed, and he places his hands on my head. As he whispers the priestly blessing, I feel his fingers trembling.

Dad makes *Kiddush*. We've arranged a buffet on the counter by the sink next to the door. My sister Sivan even tries to convince the nurse on call and the patients in the next room to join us. At the end of the meal, I kiss my dad on the forehead, and head back to Noga's parents' house.

"You're sure you don't want to eat something?" Michal asks me before I've had the chance to close their front door. I politely decline, and head to our room. Noga joins me and, like every night, one of us wraps their arms around the other. In no time at all, we're both fast asleep. And neither of us has any idea that we'll be waking up to a very different world—that our entire reality will be turned upside down—in a few short hours.

FIFTEEN MINUTES

October 7th, 2023
06:30
Ron and Tamar
The young people's neighborhood of Kibbutz Meginim

It's the early hours of the morning. I'm still fast asleep, curled up in bed with Noga. Less than a two-hour drive away, Ron, an old teammate of mine from Unit 669, is already awake — and panicking.

"Tamar, open up!" Ron shouts, banging on the door with his fist. *Why the hell is the door locked?* he thinks to himself. Nobody at the kibbutz locks their front door. Definitely not in the young people's neighborhood.

"Tamar, get up already!" The door opens a little, sending flakes of dry paint down through the air. It wasn't locked, just a little jammed. With a powerful kick, it flies open.

Tamar is sitting on her bed. Her fair hair, long enough that it reaches her shoulders, is a jumbled mess, though she's already instinctively tied it up in a scrunchie. She's wearing gym shorts and an old tank top. Her pupils contract, her green eyes blinded by the light streaking into the dimly lit room through the open door. There are still pillow marks on her cheeks.

"What are all those explosions? Is it from the festival?" she asks, her voice hoarse from sleep. "I didn't hear any sirens," she mumbles, propping herself up.

The little row of studio apartments that make up the young people's neighborhood is on the western side of the kibbutz, right up against the perimeter fence. The kibbutz is so close to the border with the Gaza Strip that rockets fired from the territory fly clean overhead—only the occasional mortar explodes within the kibbutz itself. So when the air raid siren blares, giving a short, fifteen-second warning that rockets have been fired from the Gaza Strip and are about to hit the area, it's usually meant to warn a town or village much further away from the fence. For the kibbutz residents, every siren is another round of Russian roulette. But then again, that's been a near-daily routine for the population of the Gaza Envelope for the last decade.

Ron was woken up by the explosions five minutes earlier. He too thought they were coming from a military base, or that they may have been pyrotechnics from the music festival nearby—a festival that he and Tamar decided at the last minute not to buy tickets for. Tamar and Ron are the only ones from their grade who haven't left the kibbutz yet. The rest have moved to Tel Aviv, and most are already wrapping up their degrees. Even Ron's army friends, apart from those studying medicine, have already started grown-up jobs. On the rare occasion he makes it to Tel Aviv, mostly for events of friends from the army or the kibbutz, like weddings, his old teammates always tell him, "Listen, Ron, you know what really counts in life. Believe me, I wish I had your sense. Staying on the kibbutz, living the simple life. Life here in the big city of Tel Aviv is a rat race. Who needs it?" He always nods, but deep down, he feels jealous. It feels as though all his friends have moved ahead in life, but he's stayed behind—literally—back on the ranch. He works on a dairy farm and jokes around with Thai farmhands; he spends long hours on a tractor out in the fields, toiling away just as he did at the age of fifteen—except now he's almost thirty and, on top of that, still single.

Ron's height and his mess of light curly hair had always attracted attention. He's the guy that everyone turns to look at whenever he enters a room. He's the guy who, after every wedding, is the subject of frenzied messages to the bride from her female friends: *Soo...that hunk with the curly hair and the goatee who was at your wedding...what's his name? Please tell me he's single.*

Despite the amount of female attention Ron gets—or, perhaps, because of it—it's been two years since he's dated someone for longer than a couple of months. His sisters have already given up trying to convince him to sign up for college, to try his luck somewhere outside the kibbutz. But luckily for him, Tamar also decided to stay there. Tamar is his best friend; Ron's sisters say that she's like a brother to Ron. There are photos of the pair playing in the sandpit from the age of one. Their families lived opposite from each other, so once they moved out to the young people's neighborhood, it was only natural to keep that tradition going. Tamar decided to stay in uniform after her mandatory service and continued for a few more years as an officer at the border patrol. She's not serving in the field anymore, and is about to take a break for some academic studies. She's dying to move away from the kibbutz, but she knows it will break Ron if he's the last one left there.

When the booms started, Ron had woken up in a panic, but then remembered there was a music festival nearby, and had tried to go back to sleep, without much luck. Then he'd got out of bed and climbed up onto the roof of his bungalow apartment, from which he had a clear view of the terrain beyond the kibbutz, all the way to the border of the Gaza Strip. Peering into the distance, his eyes had lingered on the vehicles streaking through the fields toward the kibbutz, uncomprehending, feeling like his eyes were sending his brain false information. Like a daydream that you know you're going to snap out of any minute, because what you're experiencing can't actually be happening in the real world. But then, he'd understood. There was no snapping out of this one.

Ron grabs Tamar by the shoulders and shakes her, his breath still reeking of sleep. "Where's your gun? There are terrorists from Gaza in the fields!"

"What? What are you…" Tamar mumbles.

Next to her bed, in the little gap between it and the slightly open window, is Tamar's army-issued assault rifle.

"Got another gun here somewhere?" he asks her, grabbing her rifle and inserting the magazine. "You took out a handgun license a while ago, right?"

Tamar nods, now wide awake. She's already wearing her military uniform and tying her laces.

"Give me a uniform," Ron asks her. He's not sure why, but it feels like the right thing. His own uniform, used for reserve duty training weeks, is in storage at his parents' place. There are no spare army boots, so he makes do with hiking sandals.

"Are you sure that's what you saw?" Tamar asks him again skeptically. Ron doesn't answer. The idea that *that's* what he actually saw is so ridiculous, even to him, that the doubt in her voice makes him think twice. Maybe it was a dream after all? A flashback to his military service. Formally, it's very easy to get discharged from the army — some junior officer that oversees HR presses a button on a keyboard, and you're a free man. But it takes years to become truly free from the army, if that ever happens at all. It has been five years, and sometimes it still comes back to him in his dreams. Especially after serving in a unit like 669.

Tamar sits behind him on the little moped. Ron revs the engine and squeezes the clutch. The tiny engine responds with a feeble whine, and they race off to the back gate of the kibbutz.

Speeding down the road to the area of the cowsheds, near the tractor shed, he pulls his cell phone out of his pants pocket, passes it to Tamar, and says, "Call my dad." The kibbutz is empty. It's a Jewish holiday today. Usually, the agricultural section would be bursting with life in the early morning. Or as his father always used to say when he woke him up for morning milking duty, in a heavy accent that hadn't changed even fifty years after he immigrated from Switzerland as a child with his parents. "The world's morning is the dairy farmer's noon."

Besides working as the manager of the kibbutz's cowshed, Ron's dad is also in charge of the local civilian defense force, a volunteer group who, in the totally hypothetical case that the kibbutz comes under attack, are supposed to be the first line of defense until the army arrives. The worst-case scenario that they've been training for over the years is that a few lone terrorists might infiltrate the kibbutz through a tunnel from the Gaza Strip, and within fifteen minutes—tops—the army would storm the kibbutz and decisively reassert control. In every exercise, every half-year, they always said: *Fifteen minutes. Hold your ground, the IDF is coming.* It had practically become a mantra.

His father answers after a single ring.

"Where are you?" he asks.

"Tamar and I are heading to the back gate. There are terrorists there. Bring us back-up!" he shouts into the phone.

"Okay, I'm trying to speak with the army. Ron, defend the kibbutz. Don't get into a gunfight if you don't have to. I bet the army will be here any minute. I'm sending the civilian defense team your way, and I'm coming."

The rifle bounces up and down on Ron's knees. Tamar is behind him, holding his shoulders with one hand, and clutching her handgun with the other. They pass by the milking parlor, when suddenly, they hear gunfire.

"Fuck! We're getting shot at!" Tamar shouts. Ron looks to his sides, trying to understand where the gunfire is coming from, loses control of the moped, and slips. The pair falls onto the road, Ron's knee crashing into a ridge in the asphalt, his rifle digging into his thigh. A sharp pain rips through his body, all the way up his spine. "You okay?" Tamar asks, groaning in pain herself.

"Yeah, I think it's just a bruise," Ron answers, gnashing his teeth. Right on the kneecap. In a second, adrenaline flushes the pain away. "We've got to find cover," he says, the sound of gunfire still ricocheting around them.

The pair crawl over to the other side of the road, toward a huge concrete block some 150 feet away. It's the base of the lamppost at the corner of the central compound of the dairy farm, a massive enclosure. They hear another burst of gunfire, followed by a terrible howl of pain from a cow. Ron and Tamar get down on their knees and hide behind the concrete block. He takes a close look at himself and Tamar, the look of a medic assessing the severity of an injury. Tamar has a deep gash in her elbow, and he's bleeding lightly from his thigh, where he got stabbed with his rifle. Nothing serious.

Ron cocks his rifle and tries to catch his breath.

The concrete block stands between them and the shooters. On the right is the cowshed, whose residents are mooing nonstop and rushing agitatedly back and forth, stomping their hooves. Straight ahead, beyond the concrete block and about 300 feet away, is the gate. The dirt road leading there cuts through the kibbutz's fields and goes straight to the border with the Gaza Strip. It's one of two entrances to the kibbutz.

Ron slowly lifts his head and peeks above the concrete block, trying to keep himself as hidden as possible. Behind the rusty gate, there are four motorbikes and a gang of people…eight, maybe ten.

You're in a dream, a really terrible dream—but it has to be a dream, Ron thinks to himself. He's overcome with fear. *There's no way this is really happening. You're about to wake up covered in sweat and stagger to the shower. You'll wash your face and head out to work. Just keep it together. This is a nightmare, it will fade away.* He clings to this thought, praying that if he focuses on waking up from the nightmare, it might just happen.

"This isn't happening. This can't be happening," Tamar repeats in shock. One of the terrorists unleashes a hail of bullets, which hits the asphalt on the road. It's early morning, the sun is yet to rise, and the two of them are already dripping in sweat, as if they were at the end of a military training day.

A white pickup truck drives through the fields and stops next to the motorbikes. In the truck bed are five terrorists, dressed in black. Their faces are covered, and each is wearing a green headband. One of them is holding a Hamas flag. Slung over their shoulders are their weapons—most have Kalashnikovs, and two have RPG launchers. One of them, the one with the flag, jumps off the back of the truck and pulls a massive pair of pliers off the back seat. He walks up to the gate and, to cries of jubilation in Arabic, clamps the device around the chain of the lock, looped around both sides of the gate.

"Tamar, how many magazines have we got?" Ron asks, giving the magazine in his rifle a light thump, making sure it's in properly. He hasn't held a gun since his last exercise in reserve duty more than six months ago, but it feels like a natural part of his body, like always. When you've fired that many rounds in your life, like any rescue soldier who has been through Unit 669's almost two-year training, holding a weapon is like riding a bike. It doesn't matter how long it's been—it's muscle memory by now.

"Two magazines for the handgun. For the rifle, only what you've got."

Ron realizes that he has to make a decision. He only has a few seconds to try to stop the terrorists. If they break the lock, nothing will stop them. Definitely not a rifle with a single magazine.

"There's no choice," he grunts and props the barrel on the concrete block. He locks the butt of the rifle into his shoulder and peers through the sight. He takes a deep breath. He's got to be precise—he has to register a direct hit, and make them think they're vulnerable. With his right forefinger, Ron gently pulls the trigger, squeezing slowly. Three bullets, all of which hit the two terrorists on one of the motorbikes. With his final shot, Ron manages to hit the pickup truck driver too.

The terrorists react with panic, shooting in every direction. Spraying indiscriminate gunfire everywhere. Ron and Tamar flinch. Bullets whizzing around them. Fragments of rock flying in their direction.

Ron takes another peek. He has to be calculated with his ammo. He knows that his mission is not to eliminate the enemy, but to keep them outside the gate. He must hold his ground until backup arrives—to exercise restraint and, most importantly, to *be precise*, because the terrorists can't be allowed to realize that they're up against only one magazine. *What the hell, where's the army?* It's been fifteen minutes. They must be in the kibbutz already, he thinks to himself; any minute, a team from the nearby post will rock up in their armored vehicles.

The rest of the terrorists ignore the two sprawled on the floor. The one with the pliers approaches the gate again. Tamar watches the whole scene unfold, pointing her handgun at the gate. Ron props himself up, squatting. He peeks over the concrete block, doing his best to peer straight down the iron sights. He fires two bullets, hitting the driver of the pickup truck and one of the motorcyclists. The terrorists crouch and start shooting everywhere again. From their shouting in Arabic and indiscriminate, sporadic gunfire, Ron picks up that the terrorists think that they're under fire from several directions. They have no clue that it's just him and Tamar, hiding behind a concrete block.

Encouraged by his success so far, Ron takes another look. He decides to try a precision shot, aiming for the terrorist still clutching the pliers.

He takes a deep breath, his target's torso right in the middle of the crosshairs, when suddenly he spots an RPG launcher pointed directly at them. The terrorist holding it lets out a cry of "Allahu Akbar!"

"Get down!" Tamar shouts, throwing herself onto Ron, and knocking him down to the ground. A sharp, whistling sound is heard, and then, immediately, a huge explosion. The RPG explodes sixty feet away, straight into the wall of the milking parlor. The dairy farm. The heartbreaking cries of wounded animals fill the air.

Tamar gets up on her knees and starts shooting. Her head is completely exposed. Trying to hit a target more than 150 feet away with a handgun is futile. Ron understands that Tamar is shooting for the sake of shooting and not actually trying to hit a target. *That's it, they're exposed.* The terrorists know exactly where they are. He props his rifle on the concrete block again, scouring through his crosshairs for the terrorist with the pliers. Tamar shouts something, but even though he is only two feet away, he can't hear a word. The gunfire is deafening. He takes a quick glance at her, to check she isn't wounded. The thought crosses his mind that even if one of them gets wounded, there's probably no better treatment than for the other one to keep shooting at the terrorists until their ammo runs out—which is going to happen in a few minutes anyway.

It looks like the terrorist with the pliers is having trouble with the lock. He shakes and rattles the chain, as if trying to break it without the pliers. Suddenly, one of the terrorists walks up to the front seat of the parked pickup truck. He pulls the terrorist Ron managed to hit out of the car, dumps him on the ground like a sack of dirt, and takes his place in the driver's seat. He shouts a few sentences in Arabic. The others stop shooting, as if they were given an order, and mount their motorbikes. They turn around, sending up a plume of dust, heading toward the path around the perimeter of the fence. They leave behind the terrorists that Ron and Tamar managed to neutralize. Tamar fires two bullets at the cloud of dust behind the vehicles as they drive off, and then—*click*, the sound telling them that the handgun magazine is now empty.

Ron sits down with a thud, plopping on the ground, his back against the cool concrete block. Tamar keeps her eyes on the vehicles as they drive off, worried they might turn around at any moment. They can hear the mooing of the injured and frightened cows through the ringing in their ears, a ringing sound caused by shooting without earplugs. "Where the hell is the army?" Ron shouts. "Is it just us under attack? Where is everyone? Huh?" he shouts, as if Tamar has the answers.

"I can't believe I'm alive," Tamar replies. "I kinda made my peace that I was gonna die here." And for the first time, she takes her eyes off the gate. Her cheeks are bright red. Sweat stains are spreading down her shirt from her neck to her chest.

"I bet they'll try to get in again through the front gate," Ron says. His knee suddenly starts hurting again. It allows itself to remember the moped accident earlier—maybe because there are no more bullets flying overhead.

Ron still can't believe that what just happened really happened. This is a scenario that nobody thought could actually happen in real life. In fact, it was so unlikely that the IDF had reduced the number of training exercises for the civilian defense teams, and even the weapons in their storehouses, despite the uproar and countless letters of protest that Ron's dad had sent to every level of the government. With all the technology and obstacles as barriers that Israel had installed over the years along the border with the Gaza Strip, everyone said that the local residents—that Israel itself—was safe from a land attack.

Tamar pulls her phone out of her pocket and starts dialing.

"You've reached the police," says a woman, clearly stressed, on the line.

Tamar presses the device to her ear. Because of the gunfire, she can barely hear anything.

Ron stands up and looks at the dirt path stretching out to the Gaza Strip, scanning for other terrorists. *The police must be inundated with calls right now*, he thinks to himself. *There is no way the police don't know that there are terrorists in Israeli territory.* Tamar also knows that, but she calls the police because that's what you're meant to do. Because that's what you're taught: If you're a civilian and you're in trouble, you call the emergency services.

During rescue missions in his military service, Ron learned that that's how people react in emergencies. Just like you're taught in first grade: *call the police.* At least, that is what people in trouble do if they can still function — if they haven't broken down or frozen.

"There are armed terrorists here, maybe ten, trying to break into the kibbutz. They're on the perimeter fence now. Tell the army to send troops!" Tamar shouts into the phone. Her voice breaks. She's not even trying to stay calm. She's just been shot at by a gang of armed terrorists, a couple of hundred feet away from her bedroom window.

Through the ringing in his ears, Ron can hear the dispatcher. "Forces are on their way. Go home and lock yourselves inside," she drones, stressed, as if she has just said the same thing on a loop over the past few minutes.

A warm wind blows through the kibbutz. The smell of dust sweeps over the fields, suffused with the sweetish scent of dung and milk that always wafts out of the dairy farm. Suddenly, it dawns on Ron. They are completely alone.

Those fifteen minutes were up long ago. Even the police are saying the army is on its way — meaning they have no idea what time they'll arrive. His mouth feels completely dry. His head is spinning.

Though he says nothing, he looks at Tamar with an expression that asks, *What the heck is going on?* Suddenly, one of the terrorists sprawled on the ground beyond the fence starts shouting. He gropes around, as if trying to find something.

Tamar instinctively picks up her handgun and pulls the trigger, but *click*—the magazine is empty. Ron feels a vibration in his pocket, a text message from his dad. *Go where the Thai workers live. Unclear what's happening there, they might need help. I've sent people to open the kibbutz's emergency stockpile. Keep safe.*

On my way, Ron replies.

He can't stop thinking about his sisters. They're so lucky they're out of the country right now, traveling, like most of his neighbors on the kibbutz.

Ron and Tamar pick up the fallen moped. Its mirrors are smashed, and the exhaust pipe has detached. Ron hands his rifle, still with a couple of bullets in the magazine, to Tamar. "I can't believe I'm going to fight Hamas with five rounds," she laughs nervously.

"It's time for you to hit a target too," Ron teases as the moped bounces up and down the potholes in the road. "Until now, I've been the only one taking down terrorists. You're just wasting ammo from your handgun."

"Screw you," she says, "we both know I'm the better shot. That's why I gave you the gun that's easier to shoot with."

They speed down to the Thai workers' living area, passing by the premilitary academy on the way. Suddenly, a thought pops into Ron's mind. "Wait a sec, what about the academy?!" He brakes with a screech. A chill runs down his spine. There are dozens of teenagers living in the building. If the terrorists have managed to break inside, they're all defenseless.

"They're home. It's a holiday, Simchat Torah," Tamar reminds him. "Come on, get a move on. You drive like an old lady, hitting the brakes every second."

They reach the Thai workers' caravans. Ron knows each of the dozens of farmhands personally. They work together in the dairy farm and in the fields. They all speak English, but they have also taught him a couple of sentences in Thai over the years.

Crying sounds ripple out of the concrete silo next to the workers' trailers, which serves as a bomb shelter when the kibbutz comes under mortar fire from Gaza.

"Help! Help!" comes a muffled voice from inside the shelter.

They run over, and Ron stops Tamar a second before they step inside.

"This is Ron! Is there anyone with you?" he asks. There might be terrorists lying in ambush inside.

"No! They shoot and run away!" he hears the voice groan. It's John, a veteran farmhand on the kibbutz.

Ron hesitates, wondering if he has another way to make sure it's not a trap. But he can't take John's cries of agony anymore, so he lunges in. There are ten people lying on the floor of the concrete shelter. Blood is draining into a dark stream along the bottom of the damp, cramped, chilly small space.

"Ron, Ron, help me!" shouts John, who recognized the voice.

It takes Ron a few seconds to gather his senses. He's never seen such a bloodbath before. The smell of blood hits him in an instant, suffocating him like campfire smoke.

Ron, he tells himself, *this is exactly what you trained for. A mass-casualty incident. You've done loads of drills like this. Focus on the ones you can save.*

He counts the casualties. While counting, he notices that some of them are not moving at all. Not breathing. The others are unconscious, but alive. Twelve casualties.

"Ron, Ron, please. Help me," John sobs in agony. Both his legs are riddled with bullet wounds. Ron feels helpless, and it drives him crazy. He is without his vest with all the medical gear, without his kit with tourniquets. Never has he come across someone injured and had absolutely no way of giving them medical treatment. He always runs up to them with a doctor or a paramedic. *All systems go.*

Suddenly, he remembers. "Tamar," he says, turning around to her, still standing at the opening of the cylinder, like there's a wall stopping her from stepping in. "There's a first-aid kit under the seat of the moped."

Half a year ago, one of the teenagers working with him in the kibbutz's gardening department, keeping the whole place freshly manicured, cut himself with some pruning shears. After the incident, Ron had put together a first-aid kit, but it was so long ago that he'd almost forgotten about it.

He takes a deep breath, the ringing in his ears subsiding, his hearing returning. He hears the sound of Tamar's boots running over to the moped, crunching on the gravel. Meanwhile, he rolls up the pant leg on John's jeans.

"Ron, I can't stand the pain."

"I'm here, John," Ron mumbles, using John's tattered leather belt as a tourniquet. He stretches the belt across his thigh, and John lets out a terrible howl of pain.

Tamar gets back with the first-aid kit—a bundle of bandages and gauze pads in a plastic supermarket bag. "Call the police again," he tells Tamar. "Tell them we've got twelve casualties here. If they don't send medical teams now, they're all going to die!"

Ron uses the only tourniquet in the bag for John's other thigh, managing to stop the bleeding from the injuries in both his legs.

Ron moves on to treat the other casualties, some still breathing, making coarse grunting noises. They're suffering bullet wounds to their chests and abdomens. The others have no pulse anymore.

"You've reached the police. My name is…"

"—There are *twelve* seriously injured people in the Thai workers' area!" Tamar interrupts the dispatcher. "When are you getting here?! Don't you understand there are casualties? Where are you? Where's the army?"

"Ma'am, the teams are on their—" the dispatcher cuts her off in turn.

"—What do you mean *on their way?* We're alone! Do you hear me?!" she screams into her iPhone. "We've got people dying here on the floor!" She chokes up. Tears welling up in her eyes.

Ron is down on his knees next to her. He sweeps his hand over the face of one of the bodies, closing her eyes. One of the female workers who joined the kibbutz only a few weeks ago.

He places his second hand on Tamar's knee, giving it a gentle squeeze, trying to give her strength.

He's trying to support her—but he also feels let down. Bitter anger spreads through his chest. It's like everything he thought he could count on, everything he was brought up to believe in, just stabbed him in the back. Police, the IDF, task forces; countless organizations that were supposed to protect them, to protect all the now-murdered people whose corpses are strewn around him; the army whose uniform he and Tamar are wearing—none of them are coming. Ron feels the anger oozing out of him, anger laced with venom. It's coursing through every fiber of his being, this fury deeper than anything he could ever have imagined feeling.

"I understand, ma'am, believe me," says the police dispatcher, taking advantage of Tamar's pause to keep talking. "I promise you, there are forces on their way. There's nothing I can say apart from *try to hold on*." Her voice sounds so weak. "There are so many casualties."

Tamar hangs up.

Ron hears quick footsteps approaching. He signals to Tamar, pointing to his ear. Tamar nods, confirming that she heard the steps. She picks up her gun and points it at the entrance of the shelter. Ron taps his fingers on his pockets helplessly, praying for a miracle and a magazine to somehow materialize there. He reaches out to John, lying between him and the opening, as if to protect him. John's eyes are closed and his breathing is heavy.

Ron's heart is thumping strongly. The sweat trickling down his face is blurring his vision. *That's it, it's over.* "If they try to kidnap us, point your gun at me and save the last bullet for yourself," he whispers. They can hear whispers outside. Tamar's outstretched arm is steady, her gun pointed ahead, her finger already prodding the trigger back. At least the first terrorist to enter won't make it out alive.

A familiar face appears at the entrance. It's David, a neighbor on the kibbutz. "Don't shoot!" he shouts, jumping back in panic and raising his arms when he sees Tamar pointing her M-4 carbine at him.

Ron feels like someone has just poured a bucket of cold water on him. He knocks Tamar's weapon off-target with a sharp flick of his hand—she's in such a state of shock that she's still pointing her gun at her parents' neighbor.

"Your dad asked me to bring you some gear." David hands them a bag filled with magazines, helmets, and a Kalashnikov rifle.

"We managed to take down a terrorist who infiltrated the kibbutz," he explains. "That's where we got the gun from." Ron inspects the rest of the kit. It's old equipment from the kibbutz's emergency storehouse, but at this point, a helicopter might as well have just swooped out of the sky to rescue them. He feels a pinch in his heart, thinking about his buddies in the unit—*where are they now? Teams from nearby bases should have joined them by now. We're on our own,* he tells himself. *But it's still us.* He looks at Tamar, smiling to himself.

"What are you smiling about?" Tamar asks him, looking puzzled.

Ron wonders whether to answer seriously but decides it's not the time to break the façade of macho cynicism. "I thought maybe with the Hamas dude's weapon, you might finally be able to take out a terrorist."

"I can't believe it," David mumbles, still standing at the entrance, taking in the scene of scattered bodies in horror.

"Sadly, there's nothing we can do for them anymore," Ron says softly. "Do you know where we need to go from here?" he asks.

"There are terrorists at the entrance of the kibbutz. Your dad said to go there." David's eyes are downcast. He can't look at the scene anymore. He feels a lump rising in his throat. He's a software engineer who works for Google. He can barely go through blood tests at the local clinic without fainting.

"Right, let's head out ASAP," Ron says, throwing the old helmet on his head. A second before they leave the concrete shelter, he kneels down again next to John. His face is pale and his eyes are half-closed. He has stopped shouting, but his whole body is convulsing in pain. Ron puts a hand on his shoulder. "John, I'm going to get help and come back. I promise." Then he picks himself up and runs over to the moped.

Ron hopes John heard him, because at this point, he's not sure he'll ever make it back — back to John, or back from this day at all.

YOU SURE THIS ISN'T A DRILL?

October 7th. 2023
07:30
Winnick, Unit 669
Tel Nof Airbase, central Israel

At the same time that Ron and Tamar are taking cover behind the concrete block on the kibbutz, at the Tel Nof Airbase—home of Unit 669—the rescue team on call are woken up by the wail of a siren.

"*Red Alert. Red Alert. The base is under missile attack,*" the metallic female voice intones, accompanied by a prolonged, unwavering alarm tone, ringing out across the entire base.

"What day is it today? You sure it's not a drill?" asks Barnea, his eyes still half-closed.

"There are no drills today, it's Shabbat. Shabbat and *Chag*.[6] Get up, move it," Winnick answers hoarsely. He pushes away the duvet cover and awkwardly clambers down from his bed, which is one bunk above Barnea's, almost landing on his bunkmate's head. The two leave the room, moving sluggishly. They head down the stairs and into the large cylindrical cement structure which serves as the shelter for the Unit 669 dorms. Before long, more sol-

---

6   *Chag is* the Hebrew word for a Jewish festival.

diers who'd also stayed on the base for Shabbat join them, including the other members of the on-call members of the rescue team. Bleary-eyed, they all squeeze into the cylindrical shelter like construction workers on a building site taking a breather and hiding from their boss.

"You guys seen that the North is under fire?" says Barnea, sharing the news from his phone. He had been resting his head on his knees as if trying to return to his abruptly interrupted dream. Winnick takes out his phone too, and sees the emergency notifications from the Home Front Command's app.[7] Instinctively, he sends a message to his family WhatsApp group: *Sirens on the kibbutz? Everyone OK?*

His skin tanned and his usual mop of curly black hair limited by the army regulation haircut to just a few dark shoots above his forehead, Matan Winnick was born and raised on a kibbutz that's less than a mile from the border with Lebanon. He joined Unit 669 after a gap year spent volunteering. A lifetime of living right on the border has wired him, in situations like this, to immediately think about the whereabouts of every member of his family. Which of them could be in the area under fire? His grandparents are living in Haifa. He keeps his eyes on his phone—his parents still haven't replied. They must have woken up his younger brother and all headed from their own beds to the guest bed in the apartment's safe room.[8] Their living room has photos of them sleeping all together

---

7   In Israel, the Home Front Command provides a civilian app that sends air raid siren alerts and updates about the security situation in the user's area.

8   All newly-built or refurbished homes in Israel now have built-in safe rooms (Hebrew: *mamadim*) which are built to protect people from missile attacks.

in the safe room from the Second Lebanon War.[9] He can practically hear his mom scolding his dad for leaving the safe room for the kitchen before the all-clear.

Winnick and Barnea, as well as the others in Cohort 48 of the unit, are due to be released from the army in a few months, finishing up almost five years of service. But in classic Israeli style, they haven't yet been informed if that will be in April or August. Either way, while the IDF is deciding exactly how many more months he needs to serve, Winnick has already started planning for civilian life. Every day, he reads books in English to make up for the gaps in his high-school education; more often than not, he was playing soccer while his friends were in class. That's what happens when you live in Uruguay for three years. Winnick's family was there because of his dad's work—and in Uruguay, soccer is as important as life itself.

With his imminent release in mind, Winnick had also decided to find a writing class. He had kept a journal for the whole of his service and had found that he quite enjoyed writing. The only one from the squad that Winnick had shown the journal to was Barnea, who had even expressed an interest in joining the writing class. "But it has to be short. Something chill, okay?" he'd added, noncommittal as always.

"Ugh, how much longer are we gonna be here?" says Barnea, his head still resting on his knees. "I think we can leave. I bet whoever's supposed to press the button for the all-clear is already back in bed. I mean, it's Shabbat morning!"

---

9   The Second Lebanon War broke out in the summer of 2006 following an attack on northern Israel by the Iranian-backed terrorist group Hezbollah. Throughout the war, towns in much of northern Israel were subject to Hezbollah rocket attacks.

Amos Barnea had also grown up in the north of Israel. He was short in stature, with thick forearms, a dense, devilish beard, and large, sparkling green eyes. He'd returned to the unit from officer training academy, where he completed his officer course—and had had a great time. The only thing he hadn't managed to do was find a girlfriend. He'd been hoping to meet someone on the course. Winnick has been trying to set him up with friends from his high school in the north, but with no luck so far. Both Winnick and Barnea are still bachelors, trying to find somewhere affordable to live in Tel Aviv.

In every group of friends, however cohesive it is, even in a cohort that is comprised of two teams of rescue soldiers going through the pipeline together for almost two years, there are always pairs and trios that are particularly close—and Cohort 48 is no different. Winnick and Barnea had become good friends early on. You might call it love at first sight; even in basic training, their commander called them "the Northern duo." When Winnick had injured his knee during a training exercise and had to have an operation, followed by extensive rehab, Barnea took it upon himself to help him get back in shape—not that anyone, including the commanders, had asked him to. He did it even if it meant coming last in the navigation exercises, or having to run more slowly in training. Barnea had always been one of the strongest of the team, both physically and mentally. He was always one of the top performers in any drill—apart from during Winnick's rehab. It was no surprise he was chosen to be sent to officer course so he could become a team leader at the unit. The two would even go to bed together: In the field, they put their sleeping bags next to each other, and in the dorms on base, they're always bunkmates.

Suddenly, loud booms echo in the distance, and the Red Alert siren starts up again. "I think we should wait to leave," says Barnea in his deep voice, his head drooped so low that it's almost resting on the cement floor. "You think those are impacts or Iron Dome interceptions?" he asks, but before someone can give their learned opinion on the matter, another siren goes off, this one rising and falling.

"Wait, is that the *rescue mission* siren?" asks Winnick, confused. The constant tone of the first siren, the Red Alert missile warning, still rings in everyone's ears.

"*Wildcats, you're on! Wildcats, you're on!*" The operation officer's voice crackles over the loudspeaker system, using the codenames for the 669 rescue soldiers — Wildcats — to announce the mission.

The members of the on-call rescue team rush out of the cement cylinder and break into a run toward the launching room. They round the gym building in a convoy, as if on a morning training run, with Barnea as the team leader. He opens up the hangar with the emergency vehicles inside. They have three minutes from when the siren went off to be on the way to the helicopter with all the necessary gear. The launching room — a huge space packed with equipment — is the unit's beating heart. In the middle, facing the main road that runs through this huge military base home to Unit 669, are two large vehicles, the unit's logo emblazoned on their doors.

Arrayed on the launching room shelves is all the rescue equipment, for every scenario you could possibly imagine. There's gear to make your way through a minefield; rope ladders and long rappelling cables; medical materials, refrigerated blood supplies, and bags with equipment for mass-casualty incidents; air tanks and diving suits; and an entire arsenal of weapons, including hand grenades, rifles, and plenty more. A rescue soldier on call can be deeply sleeping, in the middle of an intense workout in the gym or training pool, or even in the bathroom, but three minutes after the siren goes off, he has to be in the vehicle, prepared, outside of the launching room on his way with the rest of the team.

This massive warehouse is checked regularly and always fully stocked, so that whenever the on-call rescue team gets dispatched, they can throw whatever they need into the cars without delay and speed off to the helicopter, which will be waiting for them on the other side of the huge air force base.

The launching room almost functions like a reflex in human physiology. A reflex is an automatic physical reaction that doesn't need an explicit order from your brain; it's a time-saving (and sometimes life-saving) system. If you accidentally touch a hot stove, you'll instinctively withdraw your hand thanks to a reflex. Your body will feel pain, but even before the nervous signal carrying that pain reaches your brain, and even before your brain can tell your body how to act, you'll have pulled away and saved yourself a serious burn.

That's exactly how Unit 669's launching room works. Has a soldier been shot? Does a platoon somewhere need extracting? Is there a team in trouble? Have terrorists been spotted infiltrating the border? Even before the details become clear, a siren blares across the base. The doors of the launching room fly open and soldiers run through a chain of preparations on autopilot, after which, less than fifteen minutes later, a helicopter will be on its way to the scene with a rescue team on board.

"Any details on what's going on?" asks Barnea as he changes into uniform from the boxers and tank top he'd slept in.

"Something with casualties in the south, no further details," answers the operations officer, who is behind the screens in the command building across the parking lot.

The Air Force's helicopters are all over the country, on various bases. The 669 airborne rescue teams receive their deployment orders from the central command center, known as "Command" for short.

"Blood transfusion packs: moved from the fridge to the vehicles?" Winnick asks in a loud voice, serving as Barnea's deputy. His job right now is to make sure that all the necessary equipment is packed into the vehicles.

"Affirmative," Hannah, the team's doctor, and Alex, the paramedic, answer in unison.

"Devices charged up? Monitor, GoPro, night vision, respirator, blood warmer, all in the vehicle?"

"Affirmative," replies Winnick.

Winnick counts off the squad members out loud, his finger moving through the air to keep track. "Doctor, paramedic, team leader, four fighters, deputy." He points to himself last: "Barnea. All here, and we're almost at three minutes," he announces while giving a quick look at this watch. "Okay. Get in the vehicles!"

The eight team members jump into the vehicles packed with all types of gear, from rifles and stun grenades to hydraulic extraction gear and rappelling ropes for cliff extractions, and move out toward the other side of the massive Tel Nof Airbase, toward the waiting CH-53 Sea Stallion helicopters. Winnick, who's driving one of the vehicles, doesn't even bother to turn on the red siren lights on its roof. It's early morning on a holiday—the roads are deserted.

"The reports received so far are talking about a terrorist attack. Two soldiers injured," the operations officer updates the team over the radio.

"Roger that," replies Barnea.

They race over the runway and stop the vehicles by the rear ramp of the nearest helicopter. The sound of continued explosions punctuates the deafening whir of the helicopter's blades. The sky is streaked with white lines that look like chaotic contrails, which are the tell-tale sign of Iron Dome interceptions. The helicopter mechanic, standing under its accelerating blades, signals with a rapid gesture to hurry up with loading the equipment. Like a well-trained band, everyone knows their role. Barnea runs to the front of the helicopter to get the comms systems online and get more details on the mission. Winnick stands in the middle to arrange the equipment. The rest run back and forth from the vehicles, packing the huge rucksacks containing medical supplies and rescue tools, as Winnick stands at the helicopter entrance with a list, making sure that everything's loaded on. It's a critical part of the process. If something is forgotten or not packed, they won't be able to go back for it—and sometimes the success of the entire mission depends on one specific piece of rescue equipment.

"We have everything. Good to take off," confirms Winnick, within thirteen minutes of the siren going off. The pilots accelerate, moving away from the squadron building, and in an instant, the wheels leave the tarmac and the helicopters take off. Winnick looks at what's happening in the helicopter and smiles to himself, watching the four fighters from Cohort 50, the two teams of new rescue soldiers who've just finished their training and who are still freaked out by what's happening—they've only been on a couple of real-life missions. The drama of the sirens, and their immediate orders to move out, have gotten to them. He can see their anxiety from their body language, from the frenetic way they're arranging the medical equipment on the helicopter walls. Winnick remembers that feeling like it was yesterday. These days, on the brink of release and a veteran of dozens of rescue missions, he feels pretty calm and composed in the helicopter—especially with Barnea as the commander of the team on call.

He doesn't know it yet, but that composure is about to dissipate.

IT'S OPENING UP SCARS

October 7th, 2023
08:30
Guy
A neighborhood on the outskirts of Jerusalem

"I'm half an hour from base," I tell the Unit 669 coordinator.

"Great. Get here in twenty."

I get my stuff together, not forgetting my laptop. On reserve duty, they're always hurrying you, but usually there's a lot of waiting around—so I might as well be equipped to use the dead time to study and get through some work.

I make myself a coffee from the machine in the kitchen; while it's running, I have a quick wrestle with Lula, Michal and Roni's dog, who never misses a chance to play with any of us.

As I'm heading out of the house, I find Michal at the doorway.

"I made you sandwiches," she says, lobbing me a plastic bag stuffed with them.

I get into the car and drive toward the highway.

I'm speeding down Highway 1, which runs between Jerusalen and Tel Aviv, on my way to the Tel Nof Airbase.

My thoughts turn to my dad. Last night, we'd had a long conversation with the cardiologist about an experimental procedure; he had described all the tradeoffs and considerations at play, but made clear that, in the end, it was my dad's decision to make.

"Guy, what do you think I should do?" he'd asked me bluntly, just as he had at every one of the medical consultations that he'd sat through over the past week. I'd wriggled out of giving him a clear answer. He insisted that I be present at every discussion with the hospital doctors, or at least join over the phone.

I'd been meaning to speak to him about that today, to make clear that I couldn't act as his attending doctor. In any case, it wouldn't make sense medically — I'm still in school, not a doctor yet — but aside from that, we're not in the middle of the Georgian countryside anymore, and he's not in mortal danger. He's a strong man, the strongest that I know. He needs a family doctor, a cardiologist, and a psychologist, and part of the recovery process is to get comfortable going to each of them by himself, and to be capable of making his own decisions about his body. Of course, I can — I should — be by his side to hold his hand when necessary. That's what sons do. But I can't make his decisions for him.

I'd been thinking about all of this last night, and was planning to talk to him about it in the morning when I went to visit. Looks like that's not happening today, though. *I'll speak to him about it as soon as I can, once I'm released from reserve duty — probably tomorrow, maybe even tonight*, I think to myself naively.

My phone rings. I connect it to the car's Bluetooth. *Dad.*
"Hey Dad, how are you feeling?"
"Where are you going?" he asks, not answering me.
"To the unit."

"You guys got a mission?" he asks, not satisfied with my terse reply.

"Actually, no. I'm assuming that we're gearing up in case we need to transfer casualties from hospitals in the south to less full ones in the rest of the country." That actually is one of the missions that the unit would carry out. "What's up with you?" I ask him again, before he can question me further.

"Yeah, the heart's still working, though I've been better..." he says faintly. "There are sirens. It reminds me of the Yom Kippur War. It's opening up scars that are fifty years old. Guy, you and Ari, please take care of yourselves. You only just saved your dad's life. Don't rush to save your homeland too. Take your time. The war's not going anywhere."

His quivering voice breaks my heart. He's barely able to get a sentence out. *Guy, what are you doing?* I think to myself. *You should be driving east, to the hospital in Jerusalem. That's where you're needed. Unit 669 has plenty of paramedics, but you only have one dad.* I'm already stretching out my hand, ready to end the call and contact the unit, to tell them that I can't join up for reserve duty, that they should call someone else.

"Dad, what's happening there?" I ask, hearing a commotion in the background. I'm suddenly concerned.

"There are sirens every few minutes. The department is on the top floor of the hospital. They tried to move me to the hospital bomb shelter. I told the nurse I'd already been in God's waiting room three times. If He'd wanted to, He'd already have taken me. I think staying in bed and saying the Shema Prayer is safer."

I pull up to the base. I end the call, drive through the Tel Nof secured gate, and make a right turn, heading for the Unit 669 complex. *How the hell was I thinking about tell-*

ing Dad to leave me out of his treatment? I think, furious at myself. *How could I be so self-centered? The man who brought me up needs me right now, and instead, I'm off to play the hero on reserve duty.*

Still wrapped up in my thoughts, I park next to the unit launching room, where just an hour earlier, Winnick and Barnea's squad had grabbed their gear before heading out. I stay sitting in the stationary car, and a thought creeps up on me. *Did I just head to reserve duty to get away from the whole situation with my dad?*

A tap on the car window jolts me away from my thoughts and snaps me back to reality. I look up and see Itamar Feldman through the window, gesturing for me to get out of the car.

Feldman's tall, with straggly hair and a deep, resonant voice. Cool-headed by nature, it never seems to matter how much pressure he's under and what conditions he's operating in; he stays monk-like and razor sharp.

He's a religious guy, always wearing a *kippah*;[10] he spent three years studying in a religious seminary in Jerusalem. He's a couple of years younger than me, which meant that while he was in training, my teammates and I were the ones leading the different trainings in the course. Afterward, we'd served together: We'd been on a few missions together, but then, after I'd finished my mandatory service, I hadn't seen him for a few years. These days, he's studying computer science in Jerusalem and already working at a hi-tech company at the same time.

I wonder if I should tell him that I need to head back to Jerusalem; in fact, it's on the tip of my tongue.

"What's up?" he asks. "You look preoccupied."

---

10 The Hebrew word for the Jewish skullcap (*yarmulke* in Yiddish).

I hesitate for a moment, weighing up telling him the truth, but decide to hold my tongue in the end. My mom and my sisters, Eden and Sivan, are with Dad, and nothing bad will happen if I only end up going back to the hospital this evening.

Come on, focus, I say to myself. *Shake off all these thoughts for now.*

"That's your kit," says Feldman, passing me a bag of medical equipment, body armor, and a M-4 rifle.

When Feldman arrived here, just a few minutes before me, he'd been told that he was on a mission as task force commander, of a small squad of three, which apparently included me as its paramedic and Dan Shani, who had joined us too. I have no idea why they called up the three of us.

Dan is in the same cohort as Feldman, Cohort 46. Tanned skin and eyes black as charcoal, he was a lone soldier who actually grew up in San Francisco. His parents and brothers still live in California. In eleventh grade, when he and his friends, who all attended one of the top high schools in America, began the process of applying to college, he could never have imagined that within four years, he'd be a soldier in the Israeli army. His path was already set. Given his outstanding grades and his abilities as a football player, he was practically enrolled at UCLA.

But then, a trip to Israel to visit his cousins—cousins he'd never met before—turned all his life plans on their head. The two weeks Dan had spent with his cousins in Israel had been such a profound experience that by the end of them, he'd decided to enlist in the IDF. Initially, his parents were seriously against the idea, and they made their opposition clear; they also assumed that once Dan was back in San Francisco, the desire to join the Israeli army would fade away. As it turned out, they couldn't have been more wrong.

Dan's short stature and slight figure are deceptive in the extreme. I'll always remember how we discovered that Dan was more of a machine than a man. It wasn't long after his cohort had finished their training. Out of every single combat soldier, Dan was the one who had lifted the heaviest weights. He'd humbled all of us experienced soldiers—and all with his gentle American accent. We decided then and there he was made of steel. Dan's average breakfast consists of ten eggs and he works out twice a day. Even these days, when he's studying agronomy at an agricultural college and can't possibly be working out the way we used to during active service, there doesn't seem to be a single molecule of fat in his entire body.

"Where's Hasson?" I ask. That's the name on the label on the bag that Feldman handed to me, which actually belongs to a combat paramedic on mandatory service, as I had been myself until finishing up in 2018.

"Like everywhere else in the army, half of the unit is out of the country on vacation. We're in Sukkot holiday mode."

I nod and pivot to the reason we are here in the morning during a Jewish holiday. "Okay, so what's our mission then?" I ask.

"They told me to drive south," says Feldman, shrugging and gesturing to the army pickup truck nearby. "I guess we'll be given further orders on the way." The parking lot in the middle of the unit, between the warehouses and the 669 headquarters, is still almost completely empty.

What the hell is happening in the south? I wonder to myself. *And what are three guys in a pickup truck, who are used to getting places by helicopter, supposed to do there?* But for now, I decide to hold back my questions. As it turned out, even my wildest, most terrible nightmares couldn't have prepared me for what we were about to encounter.

I quickly go through the equipment I've borrowed without asking its owner. I check that the combat vest has bulletproof plates properly secured inside, and that the helmet fits snuggly on my head, and then shove everything in the back of the pickup truck. I wonder whether I should also pack some personal stuff, like underwear and a toothbrush. I'm about to ask Feldman, the commander of our tiny squad when we can expect to get back to base, but I immediately hold my tongue. He probably doesn't know—and I assume we'll probably be back tonight. I hope.

"Ready to go?" Feldman asks.

"Let's do it," Dan and I reply together. A medical student, a software developer taking his first steps into the hi-tech world, and an agriculture student—three reserve soldiers heading out, as if it were an extracurricular field trip at university.

Dan sits in the driver's seat, with Feldman next to him, and I get in the back. But not before grabbing a cup of coffee.

WE'RE ON THE WAY

As Dan, Feldman, and I are setting out from the Tel Nof junction, a helicopter is circling far above the roads leading south to the Gaza Envelope — as it has been for almost an hour already.

Winnick looks out the window. The fields, mostly just plowed earth given that it's October, stretch out underneath them. If you squint, they look like a huge, undulating chocolate cake. The view is so familiar; plenty of Air Force exercises are performed in this area, usually drills for potential rescue scenarios on the border of the Gaza Strip.

But today, something's different. Black plumes of smoke are rising up into the sky from various points. The cloudy white streaks of Iron Dome interceptor missiles still hang in the air, stretching upward like pillars of cloud. Underneath the whirring of the helicopter and the crackling comms system, Winnick thinks he can hear explosions.

"Barnea, there's another change in the info," says the pilot. "The report now is of eight seriously injured."

"Roger that," Barnea replies, and makes sure the rest of the squad heard too. It's the fourth change in the last ten minutes.

"I don't understand, why aren't we landing?" asks Winnick.

"Because there are reports of terrorists that broke through the Gaza border fence. Until ground forces get to the landing strip and secure it, we don't know if it's safe to land," Barnea explains.

"I don't get the problem," says Winnick, not letting it go. "We can deal with a squad of terrorists," he counters, impatient.

The rest of the team is following the conversation on the internal comms system. They all agree with Winnick—even Barnea, who's just relaying the logic of the commanders at the Air Force control center. All of them share Winnick's feelings, like racehorses still shut up in their starting gate, champing at the bit to be set free and rush off at a gallop.

"Dude, it's not one squad of terrorists. It's *multiple squads*. Loads of them got through the border." Barnea is starting to lose his patience.

Winnick rolls his eyes. "How many terrorists could have gotten through? The Air Force is obviously just being hysterical. Everyone knows the Gaza fence is more like a fortified wall."

Meanwhile, the pilots are in contact with central command, trying to get more information. There are reports of dozens of terrorists with shoulder-mounted anti-aircraft missiles. The casualty reports keep changing; it seems that there are multiple situations developing at the same time. It's not that the two casualties from the initial report rose to eight—there are two separate sites, in close proximity to each other, where terrorists opened fire. The command center doesn't want the helicopter landing without any protection from ground forces. What's more, if the injured aren't even at the extraction site yet, the helicopter would have to wait for them completely exposed, a sitting duck for the terrorists' rifles and rockets.

Hannah, the doctor, had been waiting for Barnea and Winnick to finish sparring over the comms system. "Alex," she asks, "given the change in the mission, is there something else you think we need to prepare?"

Hannah is a surgeon at a hospital in central Israel. In order to join the unit, she went through combat medical training within Unit 669 a year ago. This week, she's with Alex, a paramedic who's been serving in 669 for years, way before they started sending certified rescue soldiers to paramedic courses. Hannah's a doctor, of course, but she also knows that there's no substitute for the skillset of a paramedic. Ultimately, being a field doctor is a profession in its own right. As a physician in a hospital, she's not used to the harsh field conditions that combat extractions often entail.

Alex shakes his head. "I feel like we're on our way to the sort of situation you can't really prep for. We aren't going to know what's actually happening until we land."

Hannah nods, though she's unsure whether she's completely understood what Alex said.

Suddenly, the helicopter systems start to blare, and with a sharp jerk of the throttle the pilot veers to the right. The squad and the two mechanics are flung sideways like tennis balls, thudding against the walls of the helicopter's body. "There's a laser on the helicopter!" the pilot yells over the comms system. It's not the laser beam that's the problem, but what will follow: a surface-to-air missile.

The chopper's automated defense system starts emitting flares, which act as a decoy for heat-seeking missiles.

Meanwhile, in the middle of wild evasive maneuvers—
with the worst possible timing—central command gives
the go-ahead to land. The team is just a few minutes away
from its destination and the waiting casualties.

TAKE THIS SERIOUSLY

October 7th, 2023
09:30
Guy
Main highway 4, heading south

The road south is clear, as is the sky. I lie down in the backseat of the car. The newscaster on the radio is reporting on a severe security incident developing in the south. *Please follow the instructions of the security forces. This appears to be a mass-casualty incident, including hostages,* he warns, adding that *special forces are currently on their way to the Gaza Envelope.*

Suddenly, Dan slams his foot on the brakes, and my coffee spills all over my lap. I curse under my breath. "Hey guys, do you think the news presenter was talking about us? Are we the special forces heading south?"

I wipe down my pants with a roll of toilet paper I found on the floor of the car, rubbing my soymilk latte into my old uniform to soak it all up. Dan looks at me through the rearview mirror. "Dude, if he was talking about you, then we're in a really bad state," he laughs. I grimace. I hope they've sent the guys who are really "special."

About an hour later, I get a message from Noga. She had already reached her base and been briefed on the situation—or, at least, received a vague update about what the army knows at this point, which is more than I've had.

Guy, this is like nothing you've ever seen before. Take this seriously. There are terrorists everywhere. Load your magazine and cock your gun.

Yes, Ma'am, I write back, with a winking smiley emoji, before hitting the backspace and deleting the message. Maybe it's not the time to be sarcastic.

She's probably stressing for no good reason.... Then again, she usually ends up being right. I open the window, point the barrel at the sky, and cock the gun. What does she mean, there are terrorists *everywhere*? I mean, it can't be long till some military unit somewhere takes control and neutralizes them. How far could the terrorists have possibly gotten beyond the border fence?

Dan slows down. I look up from my phone. We're driving past a long line of cars parked by the roadside. They're riddled with bullet holes. Some are on fire.

"What the hell..." Dan mutters in shock, taking in the scene.

"Look!" says Feldman suddenly, pointing up to the sky through the windshield. A low-flying helicopter above the side of the road takes a sharp turn, like a jittery bird evading its pray, and suddenly flares start flying everywhere, little flames that light up the sky like a spectacular daytime fireworks display.

We reach the traffic circle. There are civilian cars riddled with bullet holes everywhere. A logjam of military vehicles blocks the road ahead. I get out of the car and start looking around, trying to understand the chaos that's broken out in the middle of this godforsaken road. We're surrounded by fields and sparse woodlands.

I hear screaming from every direction.

"I need a medic! Where's there a medic?!"

"Help me! She's bleeding here!"

"Who's got a tourniquet?!"

Total chaos. People running everywhere, completely terrified. Soldiers, police officers, and civilians. Wounded people, sprawled on the ground and bleeding, are wherever you look.

I can't get my head around what the hell happened here.

It takes me a few seconds to snap out of it and switch into paramedic mode. I quickly screen the wounded, begin initial triage on anyone I can, and then mostly bark instructions at the assorted soldiers trying to help. There are just so many casualties. I run past someone trying to resuscitate a wounded man, though from a distance I can tell that he's not alive anymore. The person straddling the body screams and cries as he continues CPR. I wonder for a second whether to stop him. I decide not to. There are bodies everywhere. *Why are they all dressed like they're going to a party?* I wonder to myself. They look like they just got back to Israel from a hiking trip through India. Maybe this was some kind of spiritual gathering? Maybe a festival?

"I need help!" someone shouts at me. I see him leaning over a young man wearing colorful loose-fitting pants, a *sharwal*,[11] and no shirt. Blood is gushing out of his thigh. I apply a tourniquet to his injury.

"You need to get him in a car and get out of here. Don't wait for help," I say firmly to the two guys carrying him in their arms. One of them is wearing a colorful headband, the other a loose and bloodstained tank top.

I hear a voice behind me shouting, "She's bleeding! Can someone come here?"

---

11   *Sharwals* are loose-fitting trousers made of cloth. They are a traditional item of clothing in Nepal.

I turn around and see a junior officer carrying a young woman. "Let me see her." Next to us is a car, parked with its doors open. "Put her on the backseat," I instruct him. He does as I say and steps aside. I lean into the car. She's a young woman wearing some colorful costume, airy strips of fabric wrapped around a bloodstained white dress. I quickly strip her down and find the source of the bleeding: a gunshot wound in her thigh, right by her hip. She's conscious—and extremely pale.

Right then, Feldman taps me on the shoulder. "Guy, we've got a mission, let's keep moving."

Are you kidding me?!

"What, now? This is a crazy mass-casualty incident!"

"We've gotta go," he says quietly.

I feel like I'm abandoning this poor injured woman.

I grab a random person standing next to me by the shoulder. "Try to apply a tourniquet to her thigh. If you can't do it, then make sure you apply pressure, and most importantly, keep driving till you reach an ambulance or a hospital."

The man nods and gets in the car. I slam the door shut behind him.

"Right, Guy, we've got to get moving!" Dan shouts at me through the driver's side window. I run over to our pickup truck and slide into the back seat, bottling up the urge to shout at Feldman that we're not going anywhere, that there are casualties here who need us. Instead, it feels like I'm sitting on my hands, doing nothing. But I'm not. I'm clutching my rifle, the barrel's pointed out of the window, and I'm instinctively scanning the landscape for targets.

Feeling like I've just been torn away from the exact place I should be right now—and torn away while there are critically injured people that need my help—I try to make sense of the chaos that we've just left behind. Screaming and shouting everywhere, cars covered in bullet holes. *Why the hell was everyone dressed like it's a rave?* I think to myself. What I didn't know at the time was that until a few hours ago, this had been the scene of a music festival—the Nova music festival—and that Hamas terrorists had massacred hundreds of people there.

Dan steps on the gas and the pickup accelerates, zooming off along the road. The whirring motor and the rush of the wind fill my ears. All I hear is panicked yelling and anguished screams echoing off each other in my head. I suddenly feel my phone vibrate. My hand leaves the end of my rifle for a moment and fishes out my phone from my pocket. *Reminder: Find wedding suit.* I look down at the notification like it's in Chinese. I can't even imagine myself wandering around Tel Aviv's shops looking for a suit with my mom. I remember I didn't reply to Noga's message. I call her. My left hand lifts up the phone, holding it to my ear, while my right grasps the handle of my rifle, its barrel resting on the frame of the car window. She's on another call.

I have to warn her. She absolutely shouldn't go south. I try calling again.

She doesn't answer. I only get an auto-reply: *sorry, not available right now.*

Call me back! I write to her.

Then I remembered that Ari went with her this morning. I call him, unsure of what I'm going to say. I want to tell my younger brother—my younger brother, who shared a room with me until I left home—I want to tell him that some bad stuff is happening here down south, and that he should stay on base. But then again, he's a commander—a great commander even, who trained and led soldiers who are now based on army outposts dotted along the Gaza border. His soldiers are on the front line of the ongoing assault from Gaza, and they're some of his best friends. If he picks up the phone and I try to stop him from grabbing a weapon and jumping into the first ride he finds going south, he'll hang up.

He doesn't answer. The phone doesn't even ring. *Shit.* I try again. Nothing.

I forward Ari the message that Noga sent me earlier, and add: *She's right! Be careful!*

"Guy, get off your phone and focus on covering the exterior!" Feldman scolds me.

I nod, admitting the lapse, and put my phone back in my pocket. I try to get rid of the thought of Noga heading south in a paratroopers' Hummer, decked out in a combat vest, the helmet on her head obscuring her ginger hair that's stretched back in a ponytail. Those Hummers don't even have a tin door like our vehicle does. *My God, please don't let her go south. Let her stay at home or on base—anywhere but here.*

The sound of gunfire suddenly rips through my thoughts. The car in front of us, a Border Police vehicle, breaks violently, and Dan manages to respond in time, slamming on our own squealing breaks. I jump out of the vehicle and try to figure out from where we're being shot at.

"Enemy ahead! Return fire!" I hear someone shouting from the car ahead of us. I crouch down, clinging to the side of our vehicle, and start shuffling forward with swift steps, staying close to the ground. There are figures in black behind a row of eucalyptus trees by the roadside, the barrels of their rifles poking out between the trees, spraying bullets our way. I run over to the car ahead of us, joining the group of soldiers sheltering behind it, and in one sharp movement throw myself on my belly and open fire toward the terrorists. I aim for the head of one of them at the edge of the row of trees. He shoots back from his hiding place and then quickly ducks behind his cover.

"Grenade!" someone yells.

One of the terrorists hurls a hand grenade our way; it falls just a few feet away, exploding with a massive blast. Luckily, it had landed in a ditch by the side of the road, so the ground absorbed the shrapnel.

The combat continues. "Terrorist down!" shouts one of the soldiers. I see one of the black-clad figures drop to the ground.

I can see Feldman and Dan a little distance away, crouching behind the barrier on the roadside. "Don't we need to get moving?" I shout at Feldman.

Feldman nods. "Get back in the car!"

"Don't get up! There might still be an enemy hiding behind the trees!" shouts the Border Police's commander.

"We've got a mission! We need you to clear the way!" Feldman replies.

"Where are you going?" he asks. The terrorists have stopped shooting, but his soldiers keep spraying gunfire at them, to make sure they are down.

"We were told to get to Kibbutz Nachal Oz."

NO SUBSTITUTE FOR A MILKMAID

October 7th, 2023
10:30
Ron and Tamar
Meginim

Back on Kibbutz Meginim, Ron gets a text from his father:

*I've logged into the CCTV from my cell phone, there
are terrorists outside the front gate of the kibbutz.
Just text your mother you're ok.*

Everyone said it was a waste of money. The Gaza border fence is a hermetic barrier. Completely impenetrable. The technology deployed along the border can prevent every possible threat. Why waste money on something as old-fashioned as security cameras when the IDF has gizmos like drones and other UAVs that can dart across the skies day and night? That's what the authorities said, brushing him off. He appealed to the kibbutz and convinced his neighbors to fork out some of their own money.

Most of them chipped in mostly because they would have felt bad otherwise, and not so much because they thought the kibbutz actually needed all this. After all, there is an army to protect them. But thanks to one stubborn, old-fashioned kibbutznik, who didn't believe that hi-tech sensors and intelligence were the solution to everything, the kibbutz installed its own security cameras. The money he crowdfunded was only enough for a few old-style cameras, but that was enough for him. As he explained the need for the cameras to his neighbors on the kibbutz, *"With all due respect to technology, even if mankind can get to the moon, if he wants milk there's no substitute for a cow and a milkmaid."*

Ron looks down at his phone, reading over his father's words again:

> *I've logged into the CCTV from my cell phone, there*
> *are terrorists outside the front gate of the kibbutz.*
> *Just text your mother you're ok.*

Well, emotions were never his strong suit, Ron thinks to himself. *Not challenging ones, anyway.* Maybe that's just as well. After all, Ron's father is the one in charge of the civilian defense squad, currently fighting the terrorists all alone. Someone better-adjusted would be torn between defending the kibbutz—the task that he's prepared for all his life—and the fact that he's sending battle orders to his own son, his "little Roni." Because his father knows that as soon as he sends Ron that message—that matter-of-fact message about terrorists at the gate, which might as well have been about a scheduled water outage—his son will head out to the front of the kibbutz, sprinting out to engage the terrorists.

That text message is Ron's father sending his son out to battle.

Got it. I'm fine. We received your gifts, he texts back. Then he sends his mom a heart emoji, and puts his phone back in his pocket before she has a chance to reply.

They park the moped a few hundred feet away from the gate, behind the kibbutz's carpentry workshop. The terrorists aren't even trying to hide their arrival. The sound of gunfire fills the air, followed immediately by the chilling sound of tires screeching and a car crashing.

"Motherfuckers," Tamar mutters, as the car plows into the roadside barrier. "They're shooting at anything that gets close to the gate. Let's get up on the roof of the minimarket. We'll have a better view of the gate from there," she suggests.

Ron and Tamar run over to the minimarket, an old one-story building that was only recently renovated. The contractor painted the flat-roofed structure in a shade of brown that reminded Ron of the kebabs from the army canteen. That paint color must have come free from the manufacturer—there was no other explanation. Behind the minimarket, there's a plastic bottle collection point, to be sent for recycling, and a big dumpster for cardboard boxes that is always overflowing.

Tamar quickly clambers onto the recycling bin and reaches out to Ron, helping him climb up to the roof. Ron's rifle clangs against the metal, making a loud crashing noise. "I get you want to tell the terrorists we're here, but at least wait till we're on the roof," she snaps at him. "Even in high school when we climbed up here to smoke shisha at night, I always had to help you up."

"If I remember right, it's your fault they caught us here in tenth grade," Ron replies.

Tamar opens her mouth to bicker about his historical inaccuracies, but then decides to ignore him. *This is an argument we can have another time.* The pair crouch down, and belly crawl across the concrete roof covered in pigeon droppings.

They hide behind the AC engine. Ron props himself up on his elbows and peeks above the metal box, watching the scene at the kibbutz's yellow entrance gates.

The motorbikes and pickup trucks they met earlier have now been joined by three more motorbikes. If the men weren't all wearing black with green headbands — and they weren't armed head to toe — they could have passed for a group of dirt bike enthusiasts revving up for a road trip. Ron counts fifteen combatants. There might be more behind the security guard's booth. "What the — " Tamar mutters. Ron feels a sharp, debilitating pain like an electric shock through his veins. His heart is pounding. He can hear his own heartbeat ringing in his ears.

Around seven hundred feet away on the road leading to the kibbutz, there's a Honda saloon car flipped upside down. The front is completely smashed up, smoke billowing out of the chassis, the windows dotted with bullet holes. It looks like the terrorists opened fire at the car once, and then took the trouble to spray it with bullets again after it crashed, to be certain that nobody came out alive.

Ron notices the terrorists gathering at a spot out of sight from the access road, behind the security booth. It's exactly where he worked just a few weeks ago with some of the local teenagers, planting snapdragons in the flowerbeds by the sides of the gate.

"What do we do?" asks Tamar. "Do we engage them from here?"

Ron shoots the idea down. "We've got no chance. We're at a bad angle, and we've only got two guns."

"Look!" Tamar grabs him by the hand excitedly, pointing into the distance, at the access road. Two military vehicles are speeding toward the kibbutz. Finally — reinforcements! For the first time, a warm feeling starts to spread through Ron's body. Backup is coming. They can hear shouting in Arabic from the direction of the gate. The terrorists have spotted the approaching cars. Maybe they've got one of their own guys observing the road. They shuffle behind the security booth, hiding to avoid being seen from a distance.

"Shit, they're laying an ambush!" Tamar says out loud. "What do we do? We need to call someone to warn them!"

The cars keep sailing ahead at top speed, blissfully unaware that just over a quarter of a mile away, a gang of armed terrorists is lying in wait. As soon as the cars enter the kill zone, the terrorists will jump out of their hiding place and slaughter them point blank.

"We can't call, there's no time," Ron mutters. His mind is feverishly racing. Two military vehicles, split seconds away from falling into a deadly trap. Two RPGs and each car will blow up with everyone inside. He feels like he is watching an impending train wreck in slow motion, and the hope he felt seconds ago about reversing it dissipates. In an instant, his whole body feels weak, helpless.

"We've got to shout something, throw some stones, something!" Tamar prods him, practically screaming.

Suddenly, an idea pops into her head.

Tamar spreads her legs open to steady her position and takes a deep breath. She expands her lungs, readying herself to shoot, and slots her eye between the crosshairs of her rifle.

"What are you doing?" Ron asks, alarmed.

She ignores him. There's no time. She sees two terrorists, still in their hiding place, aiming their shoulder-mounted rocket launchers at the approaching armored vehicles. They're armored — but only against bullets, not RPGs.

Tamar squeezes the trigger and shoots a few bullets at the first army vehicle. It stops immediately with a screech.

The second car stops right behind it, almost crashing into it. Ron picks up his weapon, aims it at the security booth at the front, shoots a few Kalashnikov bullets, and manages to hit one of the terrorists.

"Yesss! Got him," he says under his breath, as if he were talking into a PlayStation headset, trying out a new Russian-made game for the first time.

Then he turns to Tamar. "Finally you're doing something useful today," Ron laughs as the gunfire intensifies.

"You're just pissed they stepped on your flowers," she snaps.

"I really worked my ass off for those," he responds with a muffled laugh.

The terrorists step out of their hiding place behind the security hut. The pair with the RPGs stand in the middle of the road, launchers on their shoulders. Ron takes a shot at them, but without any luck. They launch their rockets, but are too far from the cars; the projectiles hit the road instead, with a massive explosion.

Soldiers jump out of both vehicles, shielding themselves behind the armored doors, and open fire at the terrorists. The gunfight continues for several minutes. At one point, they get back in their armored cars and speed toward the kibbutz, doors still open. The first vehicle stops five hundred feet away from the gate; the terrorists keep shooting at it nonstop. A grenade launcher pokes out above the open armored door and, in a second, a grenade goes flying at the security hut. One big bang, and the little building explodes with a massive shockwave, taking out the terrorists still hiding behind it.

The soldiers in the APCs don't waste a second. They race toward the gate and storm the terrorists holding out, pointing their guns right at them.

"Fucking legends!" Ron shouts, jumping to his feet and punching the air like a soccer fan celebrating a last-minute winning goal.

Tamar grabs his pantlegs and yanks him back down with a thud. "What's wrong with you?" she rebukes him, shouting, the explosions and gunfire still ringing strongly in her ears. "You're waving a Kalashnikov above your head in front of IDF soldiers that are in a gunfight with terrorists. Are you trying to get killed on the roof of a minimarket on purpose?!"

One of the soldiers has spotted Ron. "Who's there?" he barks. They all point their weapons at the rooftop — including the grenade launcher.

"Don't shoot! Don't shoot!" Ron shouts. "We're kibbutz citizens!"

They climb down off the roof and join the soldiers. It turns out they're from the Combat Engineering Corps. "They called us up, we were all at home. We got to the base and came here as quickly as we could," says their commander. "I'm Yair," he says, introducing himself and shaking Ron and Tamar's hands. "Where are all the other forces?"

Ron ignores the question and checks his watch. It's noon already.

Yair notices his expression. "Are we the first military force to get here?" he asks, astonished.

Ron ignores the question again. "But thank God you're here," he says, thinking about how close they were to dying.

Ron's phone rings. *Dad.* He answers.

"Where are you? Are you okay?" his father asks, the fear palpable in his voice. "I heard gunfire at the gate."

"I'm okay, there's a Combat Engineering team here."

"But you're okay?" his father asks again.

"Yeah, I'm fine," he says, his voice level, trying as best he can to hide the maelstrom of emotions raging inside him. He's petrified, to the very depths of his soul—partially for himself, but mainly that something might happen to Tamar, and that he won't be able to take care of her. But what else can he say to his father right now other than "I'm fine"?

He's seething with rage—at the army, at the police, at everyone. Everyone abandoned them. All those exercises and drills that his father had run over the years with the security services—it had all been for nothing. What he really wants to say to his father is that instead of running around the kibbutz, he has to go home and protect his wife, that he has to go home to Ron's mother. That he has to take care of his family. Why the hell doesn't he get that himself? He's not even capable of giving her the support of a concerned husband! He's just asking Ron to send her messages instead of doing it himself.

"Dad, everything's fine. Now what?" Ron asks, breaking his father's silence. He was back to taking orders from the head of the civilian defense team, and not from his father.

"Thank God. Roni, Chaim Moshkowitz called. Said he heard voices, people talking Arabic outside his home. I'm on my way there."

"We're joining you."

"Just tell your mom you're okay," his father asks.

Ron's about to tell his father to go to hell, and that he should be the one calling his wife, heading over to her in his golf buggy, checking that she's okay, when he suddenly hears the drumming sound of a hail of bullets in the distance. He hears it clearly through the phone, too.

IT'S NOT ENOUGH

October 7th, 2023
11:00
Winnick
The airspace above the Gaza Envelope

We leave the border patrol soldiers as they are still exchanging fire with the terrorists, and run back to our Toyota. Dan puts his foot down, and we speed off toward Kibbutz Nachal Oz.

Meanwhile, Barnea's team is lined up like sprinters in their starting blocks along the back of the helicopter hovering overhead, ready to rush out toward the injured as soon as they touch the ground.

"One minute to landing," says the captain. The stress in his voice is palpable. *If the pilots are stressed, it's a bad sign*, Winnick thinks to himself. He listens intently to the back-and-forth on the comms system, trying to work out what's going on, but it's a chaotic mishmash. Mainly, he hears tension—tension laced with panic. There's a jumble of snatched phrases from pilots in the air and staffers back at central command, but it seems like no one actually understands what's going on.

"This is a Black Hawk helicopter with thirteen strike force combat soldiers. Where can we land?"

"Identified fire toward the vehicles on the road. Repeat—"

"Negative. You're not landing. First, the Sea Stallion, going in."

"What's the situation on the ground?"

"Where's the enemy coming from? Are they here?"

"I have severe casualties..."

Winnick feels a light tap on his right soldier. Barnea is leaning toward him. He brings his mouth close to Winnick's ear.

"You're sure this isn't a drill? Doesn't feel real!" he shouts. Winnick replies with a shrug and a slight smile. Barnea's determined expression fills him with confidence. As long as they're together, everything's okay.

"We're landing!" yells the mechanic on the rear gang-plank, lowering it down. The descent takes ten seconds at most, but to Winnick, it feels like an hour. *Come on, come on, come on.* And without waiting for the mechanic's go-ahead, they all disembark, breaking into a run.

Exiting the helicopter after such a long flight, Winnick needs a few seconds to get oriented. It looks like he's on the road leading to his small hometown in the north: a two-way street riddled with potholes, shaded by a row of trees. The ditch by the side of the road is lined with dried-up shrubs. On the other side of the ditch, there's a tightly packed grove of what might be citrus trees, though he can't be sure.

Out of nowhere, he notices a stain on the guardrail. He looks more closely. They're bloodstains, more than one—and fresh. He looks behind him, past the helicopter, and sees the entrance to some small town. The yellow gate next to the guardhouse is wide open, with cars strewn across the entrance.

"Follow me!" yells Barnea, and they all move forward toward the town gateway, taking quick steps. They press on past the assortment of cars. From up close, they see that each car is riddled with bullet holes, and the glass of their windows shattered. Some of them are burnt out, others overturned—as if they'd been blown up.

"Here! I need help!"

They suddenly hear a voice from the other side of the yellow gate. A golf buggy, the type that pensioners use on a kibbutz, hurtles toward them, towing a small trailer behind it. Barnea moves toward it assertively.

"Stop!" he shouts, gesturing with outstretched arms, making sure that the cart doesn't crash into the helicopter idling behind them.

A man in a bloodstained checked shirt is sitting in the driver's seat of the golf buggy.

"Four casualties," he says, agitated. There's an armed soldier sitting next to him, his face deathly pale.

"There are terrorists on the kibbutz. We need help!" says the soldier.

"*Barnea, what's going on there?*" asks the captain over the radio.

"Check on the casualties," Barnea tells Alex and Hannah, and he starts updating the pilots.

"Four casualties. They're saying there are terrorists on the kibbutz," he barks into his radio before turning his attention back to what's happening around him.

Winnick, meanwhile, doesn't wait for further instruction. He orders two of the younger rescue soldiers on the team to spread out, scan the area for enemy combatants, and be ready to engage.

"Get the stretchers from the chopper!" Winnick tells a third soldier.

"*Barnea, I see armed men running two hundred yards away,*" says the helicopter's captain over the radio.

"We're securing the area," Barnea replies sharply.

"It's not enough! There are missile alerts and terrorists every-where. You have to get out of there," the captain shouts back.

Winnick shoots Barnea a significant look. The two know each other well. The captain's right. They have to focus on the casualties.

"He's bleeding from the neck. I need someone to apply pressure to the wound!" shouts Alex, bent over one of the injured people lying in the back of the golf cart. Winnick leaps into it, joining Hannah.

"Here, look at the bleed from the neck." Hannah shows Winnick, who pulls out a bandage from his thigh pouch and places it on the deep wound, trying to apply pressure to the blood vessel. The casualty himself is out cold. He's dressed in an army shirt, faded jeans, and white sneakers, with patchy stubble on his face. He looks like a soldier on leave. Almost immediately, Winnick's hand is covered in the blood that's gushing from the wound. The stench of charred flesh fills his nostrils.

"Move the injured to the helicopter!" shouts Barnea, and the team immediately hoists the casualties onto stretchers and runs back to the helicopter. The mechanic raises the gangway and they take off, heading for the hospital. Winnick's hand is still on the wounded soldier's neck.

"I'll apply pressure on the wound, give him blood!" Hannah shouts in Winnick's ear.

Winnick nods, places an IV into the casualty's fore-arm, and attaches a blood transfusion pack. His powerful arm starts working vigorously, pumping blood from the pack straight into the patient's vein. Sweat rolls from his brow down into his eyes, but he doesn't look away for an instant. He pulls the syringe handle, turns the valve, and injects into the vein over and over again, emptying the entire bag of blood into the casualty's body. Winnick notices that he's regaining consciousness: his eyes have started to flicker, and his face is contorted in pain.

The helicopter hits the ground with an abrupt bump. The green grass visible through the windows signals their arrival at the landing pad at Soroka Medical Center, in the southern central city called Be'er Sheva.

The squad runs out carrying the stretchers. They set them down onto the hospital's electric buggies, leap in themselves, and set off for the trauma room, where the hospital team is supposed to be waiting. That is the regular drill when a 669 helicopter lands at the hospital.

"What the hell is happening here?" Winnick mutters as they enter, letting his thoughts slip out through his mouth. There are injured people everywhere—sitting on the waiting room benches and groaning, leaning on the doorways of the entrance, with many still lying on the ambulance beds on which they'd arrived. Cries for help come from every direction. Nurses are running around, trying unsuccessfully to impose some order on the situation. With what feels like every passing minute, there's another casualty being rushed into the trauma room.

"He has to get a CT!"

"Where's there an orthopedic surgeon? I need an orthopedic!"

"Who's dealing with the casualty that was just brought in?"

"We're losing him; where's the anesthesiologist?"

The team gives details on the casualties they brought in to one of the hospital doctors.

Winnick feels like he's suffocating, like his oxygen supply is being cut off by the growing mass of human chaos that's filling up the room. He desperately wants to get out into the open—and besides, they should give the hospital staff some room to work. They're doing their best to process and treat what seems like an endless number of casualties. A rescue team right in the middle of the room, laden down with gear and supplies, is the last thing they need.

"I'm heading out to get some air," he says to Barnea as he passes him, and, without waiting for a reply, he heads through the double doors separating the trauma room from the emergency room.

Winnick puts out his hand to open the door—and then stops where he is. He notices a lone hospital bed by the wall. There's a figure lying on the bed, covered head to toe by a hospital blanket. The only parts of the figure's body protruding from under the blanket are the soles of the feet—in fact, the soles of hiking boots. They're the exact same boots Winnick's wearing now. Hiking boots that the army issues to soldiers in special ops units.

Winnick suddenly gets the urge to pull off the blanket, just a little, so that he can see the face. *You have to make sure it's not someone you know*, he thinks to himself. He stands motionless for a few moments, his hand still on the door as if it's been frozen and is stuck on its white surface. He suddenly has a blood-curdling thought: *What if it's Yaniv or Yuval, his friends from the co-op he was part of during his year of community service? They both serve in the Duvdevan unit together; they were both recently issued with boots just like those ones. Or it could be Erez, his childhood friend—navy commando fighters get those boots too.*

Winnick goes through the list of friends running through his head, trying to rule them all out. He looks at the length of the body. It's about as long as the bed itself—that fits with how tall Erez is. Winnick remembers suddenly that Erez had told him that he hadn't gone home from the army for Simchat Torah, that a friend on his team had asked him to swap weekend duties.

Winnick's eyes are transfixed on the top portion of the hospital bed, almost spellbound. He makes out the shape of a nose between the folds of the pillow. It looks like Erez's arched nose, the nose he broke playing soccer in fourth grade. Winnick, in a trance, sees Erez's brown eyes looking back at him from under the blanket, shining as always, glinting mischievously, watching him, waiting for the perfect cue to fling off the covers, leap up from the bed, and roar with laughter. *"I should have got a picture of your face. You really thought I was dead, huh?"*

He starts feeling faint. He moves away from the hospital bed, his body filling with dread. *Calm down, everything's okay*, he tells himself. *It's a body, but it's not Erez. Get a grip and move forward.* He swallows, screws up his eyes, forces his gaze away from the hospital bed, and exits the trauma room.

Winnick sits down on one of the benches in the bustling corridor, trying to regain control over his breathing and his thoughts. His face is covered in cold sweat. His thoughts are still on Erez, unsure whether his vision had been real or just a dream. In front of him, people are in constant motion, medical teams rushing back and forth; but Winnick feels utterly alone.

He pulls out his cell phone from his pocket, intending to call Erez. Winnick can already hear his friend's high-pitched voice: *"What, you thought I died? You think I'm gonna let some piece of crap terrorist kill me? We had an agreement, I told you — I'm gonna die trekking in the Andes mountains in Peru!"*

Winnick unlocks his phone and sees a message in his family chat. The adrenaline of the rescue mission had distracted him from his concern for them, but now it comes flooding back. He opens WhatsApp straight away.

"We're OK. There are sirens, but everyone on the kibbutz is OK." He reads the message from his parents and exhales

deeply. There are a ton of WhatsApps from friends too, asking if he's okay.

Winnick looks over the messages, wondering why everyone is worrying about him. If none of his exes had messaged, then it can't be that much of an emergency. *That's what Erez would say*, he thinks, smiling to himself. Intending to give Erez a call, Winnick absentmindedly opens up a WhatsApp group of his army friends. It's packed with videos. He hits play on one. A truck full of terrorists drives along a road, in what looks like a neighborhood of an Israeli town. He plays another. An IDF soldier, unconscious, on the back of a jeep, is being carried through the streets of what looks like an Arab city. A half-naked young woman, covered in blood. Terrorists shooting into the air on the grassy lawns of some kibbutz. *No. No. This cannot be happening.*

Winnick lifts up his head and sees people gathered around a TV mounted on the corridor wall. He joins them, peering through the crowd of people to make out what's happening on the screen.

The banner headline at the bottom of the screen makes his blood run cold. His mouth goes dry. His heart starts to pound violently.

"What the hell is this?" he murmurs.

More than 100 dead—Hundreds more injured and missing—Suspected hostage situation.

The phone in his pocket rings. Barnea is calling.

"Yup," Winnick says, his eyes glued to the TV.

"Get to the helicopter now. We're taking off for another mission."

WORKING FOR ELON MUSK

"The mission: to go house to house, building to building, and liberate the kibbutz," says the company commander tersely. He's standing in the middle of a patch of pine trees on the outskirts of the kibbutz, above which there's smoke trailing high into the air. "Take a drink of water, check your guns and ammo. Two minutes 'til we go in."

Standing in a semicircle, dozens of other soldiers and I nod and disperse, each busying themselves with whatever feels most important to do before entering the kibbutz. It's noon, and the air around us is stagnant, clammy even. We hear gunfire from neighboring kibbutzim—or maybe, it's actually coming from inside the kibbutz right in front of us. Who knows. Here and there, there are echoes of massive explosions: tank shells.

I adjust my army backpack and tighten the strap of my helmet. With the time that I have before we enter the place, I decide to try calling Ari and Noga again. I take out my phone from my pocket and see that the battery is already half-empty. *Why the hell didn't I charge it during the night?* I try to place the call, but I can't get any reception. *How is that possible?* I think to myself, annoyed. *We're on the edge of town.*

"Guy, enough with the emails, leave your phone. Check your magazines are loaded. We're about to head in," says Dan, who's standing beside me. He looks like a raging pit bull, ready to attack.

"I can't get a signal. I'm turning it off and on again," I reply irritably.

"Turning it off and on again. Remind me what you do in life? Can't believe Elon Musk hasn't recruited you yet for his tech department," he says with a smirk. "Come on. Focus. Pull yourself together. Be ready for the mission."

I return his smirk, and go back to staring at the screen, hoping to see some indication of a cell signal pop up. It's true that I'm often on reserve duty—and when I am, I'll carry out helicopter rescues and treat the injured—but I definitely can't say I feel ready for this particular mission. What I "do in life," as Dan put it, hasn't prepared me in any way for something like this. Liberating a town that's been invaded by Hamas. All-out combat with a terrorist invasion force. God only knows what's waiting for us on the other side of the kibbutz fence. I'm a medical student. I study for tests, do some medical research, write for a newspaper, and hang out with friends at Tel Aviv bars. I'm busy with wedding planning. I spend most of my waking hours in front of a laptop screen. How the hell have I ended up here?

These thoughts all whirl round my head at breakneck speed, each one compounding my stress levels. My fingers grip my rifle even tighter, like they're trying to crush it. My shoulders are tensed.

I'm suddenly reminded of a conversation I had with my father, years ago. It was just after I'd finished my army service and started studying for the psychometric tests. I told my father how worried I was about not being accepted to medical school. What chance did I have of getting a good enough score on the test? In high school, I'd been a pretty average student.

"Sometimes I think about that when I'm lying in bed, and it takes me hours to fall asleep. Or I'll wake up in the middle of the night, suddenly thinking about my studies, and I can't get back to sleep. It's really weighing on me," I told him.

"Hey, Guy, what are you doing right now?" he had asked me, after I'd finished explaining.

"What do you mean? I'm talking to you on the phone."

"Okay. What else, apart from speaking to me on the phone?"

"I'm sitting, waiting for the bus."

"Does anything hurt? Any part of your body?"

"No..." I'd replied, hesitantly, not really understanding what he was getting at.

"So—you're sitting down. You're talking to your dad. I'd guess you're also breathing. The sun is shining. And you're physically healthy," he'd said, as if coming to some grand conclusion.

"Err...sure. That's right," I'd mumbled in reply.

"So what's there to worry about? Everything's okay. Whenever you think about the psychometric test, and you start to get stressed and lose control of yourself thinking about the future, just come back to the present." He'd said this in the tone he reserved for the insights he'd gained from practicing Buddhism.

I remember my initial response to all that: *Oh, come on. Enough with all that new age crap.* But even so, every now and then, I try to apply his technique.

Guy, I think to myself, *you're standing straight. You're healthy. You're with good people that you can count on. The sun's out. When the difficult moment comes, you'll be strong. But right now, everything's okay. Just keep breathing —*

"All right, let's move!" the company commander growls, interrupting my mini retreat and snapping me back to the glade outside Nachal Oz. He starts walking, and we follow in a long line.

As we make sure to keep a few feet between us, I realize that I haven't walked in combat formation in years, maybe even since my basic training. I feel like I'm in a surreal dream. Marching into a kibbutz with an armed company. Sent into battle carrying a gun that I've never even tried at a shooting range.

Our column enters through the yellow gate, down the main road into the kibbutz. Decorative wooden signs point visitors to sites around the community. The ornamental trees and flowers in the gardens remind me of the entrance to Kibbutz Ramat Yohanan, where I was born. I look around, my eyes darting, searching for any suspicious movement. In every window of every building, there could be a terrorist pointing an RPG at us. As we move through the kibbutz, the fear gives way to confidence. It must be some kind of physiological calming reaction.

Suddenly, a massive explosion rips through the air.

Instinctively, I duck and raise my rifle to my shoulder, cursing under my breath. A mortar shell comes crashing down, sending a plume of dust into the air a couple hundred feet away.

We scurry over to the first row of houses. It looks like a new neighborhood. The lawns are still symmetrical, laid out in perfect squares on the front yards. My whole body is tensed up like a tightly-wound spring, ready to unfurl at the slightest movement. Thick smoke billows out of one of the buildings. Just a few steps away from us, there are bodies sprawled along the road. Five terrorists. Thick beards and green headbands with Arabic writing on their foreheads. Camouflage pants and black vests packed with ammunition, Kalashnikovs and RPG launchers lying next to their bodies.

I stare at them for a moment, just to make sure they've really been neutralized. They must have been taken down by members of the kibbutz. I can also see the bodies of Israelis. It's too easy to tell the difference. I walk up to them and pause briefly, checking if there's any chance of saving anyone, but one quick glance at their horrific injuries is enough. There's nothing we can do for them anymore.

A primal, feral dread creeps up my spine. It's a type of fear that I haven't felt in years. The silence around us feels artificial and eerie. At any moment, a burst of gunfire could pierce the air, and before we even know where he's shooting from, a terrorist could take us all down. We'd instantly join the dozens of corpses scattered all around us. I don't think I've been this terrified since my mandatory service days.

Actually, even then, I never felt the sheer terror I do now. Even when I was in a dangerous place or situation, I think my walls of denial had been thicker. Things had felt more like a game, a super-realistic drill—there hadn't been space for fear. I'm analyzing my own psychology, giving my thoughts somewhere to go. Better they turn toward psychology rather than focusing on the corpses and pools of blood all around me. I keep scanning from side to side, my eyes wide and bulging. I'm definitely not in a drill. There's not the slightest doubt in my mind that this is real—it's all too real. That became crystal clear a few hours ago. And if this is a drill, I'm definitely not equipped to deal with it.

We take a turn, onto a path that leads from the road to a row of houses.

From nowhere, gunfire opens toward us.

"Ambush! Ambush!" yell others from a nearby building.

"I see two terrorists. Building to our west," I hear someone shout. I can't see the terrorists and I'm worried that I'll shoot one of our own guys. The sound of automatic fire from a Negev light machine gun rips through the background. The addition of automatic Israeli weapons to this gunfight fills me with optimism for some reason.

Suddenly, I see the terrorists running, scrambling out of a building that was, until a few hours ago, a family home. They're trying to escape through the back door, from what looks like a utility room. Instinctively, I swiftly kneel, shove my eye into the eyepiece, aim toward them, and start shooting. Two more soldiers target them with close-range fire from a nearby building. With a few precise shots, the two terrorists are down.

One of the terrorists manages to spray bullets everywhere before going down. He screams and drops to the ground. The soldiers nearby shoot him, to be sure that he's neutralized.

"Hostiles neutralized, incident over," says the company commander. "Sweep the building they came out of," he orders a group of soldiers nearby.

"Where's the paramedic? We have a casualty!" someone shouts. I run over.

"I took a round to the chest," mumbles one of the soldiers who shot the terrorists. He points to his side, with panic in his eyes. Rapid breaths. He has a hole right under his armpit.

Treating a casualty between terrorist-infested buildings, or right next to frightened families taking shelter in their homes, is far from ideal—even less ideal than a clearing in a forest. So two guys help the injured soldier limp over to the woodlands right outside the kibbutz, where the company's Hummers are parked.

Feldman and I help the injured soldier sit up on the stretcher; it's easier to breathe sitting than lying down. I ask one of the soldiers to strip him down.

"What's your name?"

"Amichai," he pants.

The terrorists managed to hit him. The entry wound from the bullet is unmissable. It went straight through a gap in his body armor, but it didn't go out the other side. There's a large bump around his left shoulder, on the opposite side of his body from the place where the bullet flew in.

"How do you feel?" I ask Amichai and pop a needle in his vein.

"It hurts…hard to breathe…you don't need to be a paramedic to diagnose a chest injury," he chuckles, which costs him a cough full of blood. I poke the needle into a prominent vein on his muscular forearm. He has fair eyes and a faint mustache along his upper lip. I take his helmet off. His hair, drenched with sweat, clings to his forehead.

"How do you know what a chest injury is?" I ask him. "You a medic, by any chance?"

"Yes, I'm a medic. Hang on," he says, looking at me, "I know you. You gave us a lecture during our training course!" He coughs again. "What are you doing here?" I smile and give him a lollipop with a strong painkiller. I'm asking myself the same thing.

"When are we getting him out of here? I need a helicopter now!" I shout at Feldman. In the corner of my eye, I see him pacing up and down, trying to make contact with someone through the radio device.

"No answer yet," he says, frustrated. "Not on the phone or the radio."

"What do you mean they're not answering?" I fume. "We're in the State of Israel. Get me any sort of medical transport to get this soldier out of here!"

"Oh really? Thanks for the explanation, now I understand," he snaps back, my frustration triggering his own.

While we wait for an update from Feldman, I try to get a sense of the injured medic's condition.

"How do you feel?" I ask him after a few minutes.

"Better," he replies. He looks less frightened. The lollipop is doing its job. But I have to yank it out of his mouth.

"Sorry, bro. I want you to be able to sit up. Suck on that too much, and you'll have to lie down," I explain. He smiles with a dopey nod and breaks into a chesty cough, spitting out flecks of blood.

"Tell me, Amichai, what are we worried about? What's the worst that could come out of an injury like yours?" I ask him, like we're running a training exercise in a classroom. Understanding what's going on, and the nature of the injury, instills confidence in a casualty, especially if he understands medicine. But I guess the real reason for my pop quiz is that if I don't distract myself, I'll probably start punching someone in fury. How is there no evacuation vehicle on its way?

"Tension pneumothorax," Amichai mumbles.

"Very good. I think you've earned a prize." I pop the lollipop back in his mouth. He's conscious, and his blood pressure is normal, but I'm really worried about his condition—it can flip in a matter of seconds without warning.

Feldman walks over to me, looking downbeat. "No comms. Nobody's answering. Can't get them on the phone, not even on the radio."

I feel anger welling up inside me. How the hell is this possible? I look around. What are we doing here? I stroke my stubble with my fingers. I've got a terrible idea. I mean, horrifically negligent from a medical perspective, but I can't see any way out of it.

"Who here can drive one of these Hummers?" I ask the soldiers around me. One of them raises his hand. "What's your name?"

"Hercules," he snarls quietly. Not a bad nickname for a guy with shoulders the width of a Hummer.

"Listen," I say, and signal for him to come closer. "Amichai has a chest wound. We're going to seat him in your car and you're going to drive as fast as you can till you reach an ambulance or a hospital. Until you see one of them, don't stop. Even if you come under fire, you keep driving till —"

The deafening explosion of a mortar shell cuts me off, crashing into the adjacent field. Instinctively, I protect my head. As if covering my helmet with my bare hands will do anything.

"What do you mean? Won't you be sitting in the back with Amichai — ?" asks Hercules.

"No, nobody at the back," I cut him off sharply. "We don't have enough medical staff. We're still in combat. It's you, Amichai, and the accelerator. Got it?"

"What do I do if his condition gets worse?"

"You hit the gas harder."

Hercules nods hesitantly.

We help Amichai get into the Hummer. I confiscate his lollipop again. I can't believe that I'm evacuating a casualty with a bullet in his chest in the back seat of a Hummer, without medical treatment, without monitoring him, like a grocery delivery from the supermarket. I hand Amichai his helmet.

Hercules revs up the engine and drives off. I hang around for another couple of seconds, watching the car disappear down the dusty path down to the main road. I'm still slightly shocked by the decision I just made. Little do I know, this is nothing compared to the decisions I'll soon need to make.

I look around. Pillars of smoke are still billowing out of the fields. Suddenly, I hear gunfire inside the kibbutz. I feel a sense of desertion, as if we've been thrust into chaos, and there I am, all alone in the world.

A GREEN PARADISE

October 7th, 2023
13:00
Ron and Tamar
A neighborhood in the North of Meginim

As we continue going door-to-door at Nachal Oz, back on Meginim, Ron directs the army forces around the winding paths of his kibbutz.

"Take a right at the traffic circle, and then straight after the row of carob trees, take a left," Ron instructs the combat engineering soldier in the driver's seat. They are driving through the kibbutz, the massive vehicle juddering up and down on the narrow paths paved for bicycles and mobility scooters, crushing the flowers and hedges adorning the sides of the paths with its heavy tires. Ron is deliberately taking them to the furthermost neighborhood, on the edge of the kibbutz, where Chaim Moshkowitz heard voices and then gunfire; down the narrow country lanes and not along the wider perimeter road. This way, they can surprise the terrorists who infiltrated the kibbutz while avoiding being ambushed themselves. In any case, his father already told him that he was on his way with guys from the civilian defense team via the perimeter road.

Ron knows that his father has sent him down the less dangerous route, even though he's the one with a squad of soldiers and two APCs. His father and his civilian defense buddies will be exposed to gunfire on the bypass road in a white buggy that would look more at home on a golf course.

His mother had updated him that she'd moved over to the neighbors' house, to their safe room, so as not to be alone. She'd called in the morning, and when he hadn't answered, she'd written:

> *"I won't bother you. Take care of yourself, and of dad. I need my husband and my son, not heroes. Please, think of me."*

Thanks to her considerable level of emotional intelligence—without which she never could have survived in a relationship with his father—Ron's mother is managing to limit herself to one message an hour. She lets him know she's okay, and he replies with a heart emoji. Ron and his mother have a strong relationship. Tamar always says she's jealous of him, that she would want a mother like his. "As well as my mom, not instead!" she'd always been sure to clarify.

Ron's father had never had a mom or a dad. Not because they'd passed away—they're still alive and live close by in the outskirts of Be'er Sheva—but because they'd lived on a kibbutz. At the time, most Israeli kibbutzim practiced collective childrearing. Ron's father hadn't grown up with his parents, but in the communal children's house. Parents were only allowed to spend an hour or two each day with their child; in the afternoon, before the children all went back to the children's house with their caregiver to wash and eat dinner. There had been ten children his age on the kibbutz: nine boys and one girl. In a sense, they'd all brought each other up.

Ron had understood from an early age that his father's capacity for expressing emotion was severely limited—like a clock with no numbers around its face. Ever since he'd been a schoolkid, and all the way through his army service, Ron had always shared everything with his mother. Conversations with his father, on the other hand, were pretty terse. "How are things?" he'd ask. "All good," Ron would reply. He goes to his father for practical things, like if something needed fixing or building.

But when he needs someone to listen, he goes to his mother. She always takes care to say the right thing in every conversation, and she always gives good advice regardless of the situation. Even these days, when he's feeling like his life is at a dead end. When he finds himself sitting alone on his beaten-up sofa outside his room in the youth dormitories of the kibbutz, and he starts feeling overcome by depression, he'll pick up the phone to his mother. *She's probably checking on all the neighbors right now*, Ron thinks to himself, *making tea, calming them down.*

"Here on the right, you'll see a sign in a second. Stop there." Ron points at a row of cottages with red-tiled roofs. There's nobody in sight. For hours, everyone on the kibbutz has been hiding in their homes. He knows who lives in each house. He can see movement in the windows, figures moving around. He hopes that the sight of a fearsome military vehicle plowing its way down the path in front of the houses will give his neighbors some hope.

The driver stops in front of a wooden sign, etched with the words: MOSHKOWITZ FAMILY.

"Right, let's get out," snarls Yair and jumps out of the car, engine still running, followed immediately by all the other soldiers. Yair takes a skeptical look at Ron and Tamar, checking them up and down. His soldiers are well equipped; those two are wearing filthy uniforms covered in pigeon droppings from the roof of the minimarket and old oversized rusty helmets. They look fresh out of a World War II movie, with green cooking pots on their heads.

Tamar notices his expression. "Kibbutzniks don't need fancy gear," she quips with a smile and a wink.

"Gather round," asks Yair, and they stand by him. He raises his voice to be heard over the engine. "The man who lives in the house behind me called and said he heard noises, and since then, he hasn't been answering the phone. Don't let this green paradise of trees and flowers deceive you. We're in urban combat," he says, almost as if to remind himself, between the incoming rockets from Gaza, Iron Dome interceptions, and IDF fighter jets flying overhead. Flocks of birds chirp in unison from the treetops. For a moment, Yair feels like he's at his parents' home in a village near the Sea of Galilee. He shakes it off.

"Okay, let's get moving."

They advance in a column, skirting around the house, walking slowly along the wall. A narrow strip of grass separates Chaim Moshkowitz's house from that of his neighbor to the north. Leading the force, Yair reaches the corner of the house and turns around slowly with his weapon ahead, peeking around the wall. He swerves nimbly around the corner, like a razor blade delicately flicking open.

In the backyard of the house, there's a wooden pergola covered in palm fronds for the Jewish holiday of Sukkot, with colorful paper decorations hanging from the poles. Inside the structure, there's a low glass table covered in plastic toys, and a set of plastic chairs. A ginger cat stalks the veranda, quickly dodging the group of soldiers. Yair doesn't sense anything suspicious; the backyard seems completely quiet. Maybe too quiet. The kibbutz fence is about three hundred feet away. It's basic metal fencing —

not a particularly complicated obstacle. Beyond it, you can clearly see the Gaza border.

Yair slowly opens the side door that leads out into the backyard.

"IDF!" he shouts as they step into the living room, so that anyone in the home won't think that they're terrorists. Inside are two light blue sofas positioned in front of an old television. Behind it are wooden shelves, overflowing with books, themselves punctuated by framed family photos. The faces of Mr. Moshkowitz's children and grandchildren, as well as that of his late wife, who died two years ago, look down on them. The pungent smell of spices fills the air. Many years of home cooking have suffused the walls, infusing the aromas into the concrete and cement.

Yair spots a dark stain sparkling on the floor tiles behind the sofa, when suddenly a black-clad figure leaps at them from the hallway, screaming "ALLAHU AKBAR!" and opening fire. The first hail of bullets hits Yair, who manages to return fire and hit the terrorist, right in the head. The terrorist collapses in the middle of the living room. Within seconds, all the other soldiers start shooting at the jihadist, who's lying on the floor, still making gurgling sounds.

"Go down the hallway, sweep for other tangos!" shouts Ron.

Tamar and three other soldiers run to the corridor that the terrorist jumped out of. Ron kneels down and places a hand on Yair's neck. A reddish hole with rough-hewn edges, blown through his gentle face. Right under his jawbone. His big, green eyes are wide open. Ron can't detect a pulse. No movement in his chest. He passes his hand over Yair's eyelids, over the handsome face whose eyes will never open again.

"All the rooms are clear!" Tamar shouts down the corridor. The three soldiers — Yair's men — look at Ron. Their eyes reflect confusion mixed with panic. Ron grabs a thin woolen blanket from the sofa and covers Yair.

"What about him?" asks one of the soldiers, pointing at the sofa. It takes Ron a second to remember. Behind the sofa, right under the table, all set with a festive white tablecloth, adorned with the etrog and lulav for the last day of Sukkot, lies Chaim Moshkowitz, a red stain spread across his shirt, his wrinkled face as pale as plaster. He is panting heavily.

"Help me flip him around," Ron asks one of the soldiers. He performs a visual scan of the old man's back and the upper part of his legs, searching for another point of injury apart from the gunshot to his abdomen. Chaim is unconscious; his body is drenched with sweat, as though someone had poured a whole bucket of water onto him.

"What's going on? Who are you?" Ron's father bursts into the living room, together with two of his neighbors. They are clutching old civilian defense weapons, with those upside-down cooking pots on their heads.

"Dad, these are the guys from the Combat Engineering Corps," says Ron. "A terrorist ambushed us. Chaim is still with us, but he's seriously injured. We need you to take him to a hospital right now." His father's eyes wander over to the sheet covering a figure on the floor. But Ron answers him with a subtle shake of his head: *Don't ask.* They lift Chaim, wounded and groaning in agony, and place him in the container of the golf buggy.

"We'll take him to the gate. We'll find a way to get him to the hospital in Be'er-Sheva," says Ron's father, but his voice makes it clear that he has no idea how to actually do this. Terrorists are lying in wait around every corner and the whole kibbutz is off-limits to medical teams. "Call your mom, she's worried about you!" he shouts at Ron, and slams his foot on the accelerator of the golf buggy.

Silence. Ron looks at Yair's soldiers, standing around the body of their late commander, covered in a sheet. Twelve soldiers, some looking straight at him through teary eyes, others averting one another's gaze as if looking for something to distract them. One of them takes a tea towel and covers the face of the terrorist lying in the corner by the corridor. Ron thinks they look lost, like they're waiting for someone to tell them what to do, what their next moves are. One of them reminds Ron of how Unit 669's psychologist described a soldier suffering acute stress disorder during combat: disquieted, his eyes staring into space, swaying from side to side, sitting on a chair he brought over from the kitchen, tapping his fingers on the petals of the flower on the vase on the table.

"Guys," Ron says, cutting through the silence. "I'm really sorry." Silence again. It's like there's a heavy blanket covering the living room, muffling every sound, despite the shooting and reverberations of explosions all around them. "I'm guessing most of you, if not all of you, have never been here. You probably don't know anyone here. You don't even know anything about me besides my name, and we've been fighting together. I don't know what will happen from now on, but it's important for me that you know — you saved us. You and Yair, leading the team, saved me today, saved my family, and saved the residents of this kibbutz."

Ron has never been much of a talker. He has a habit of blushing and stumbling on his words. But as he speaks, he feels like the words are coalescing into sentences by themselves. "Thank you for coming," he says to conclude and looks down at his feet.

One of the guys, the one who covered the terrorist with a towel, shuffles toward Ron and places a hand on his shoulder.

"We're here for you. For all of you. Tell us where we're going next."

Ron nods. They head out of the living room. On the step of the house's back porch, he notices a picture of his mom and Chaim's late wife. The two were very close friends. In the picture, the two women are with a few kids and an Arab-dressed woman, sitting on what seems like a hospital bed. He gazes at the picture for a few seconds, suddenly recalling that the two of them were part of a group of volunteers who drove ill people from Gaza to Israeli hospitals on a weekly basis, so they could get better treatment than what the hospitals in Gaza could offer.

He remembered that, at one time, a few years ago, during one of the rounds of missile shooting from Gaza, he got mad at his mom because she insisted on going to the border to take the group to the hospital, as she did every week, although every few hours, there were Red Alert sirens going off and missile shooting all over the south.

"You think the families of the patients with cancer you are taking to Sourasky Hospital in Tel Aviv today would have done the same for you?" he asked over the phone, not hiding his anger.

"You know I don't think so Ron. I am not that naïve," she answered quietly. "But that is the point of doing good; doing a Mitzva, you don't expect anything in return."

Ron gives a last look at the body of the terrorist lying on the floor and walks out to the garden that looks toward Gaza and returns to their vehicles on the narrow path outside the house.

Tamar, who had hung back for a moment, jogs out to catch up with them.

"You're okay?" asks Ron.

"I had to turn off the hotplate in the kitchen," she replies, and gets into the car.

IS HE STILL ALIVE?

October 7th, 2023
14:00
Guy
The rear entrance of Kibbutz Nachal Oz

"Casualty arriving!" shouts one of the medics. I shake myself away from thoughts of Amichai, borne away by Hercules to who knows where, and jerk back to the present. Four soldiers carrying a stretcher sprint toward us. "Civilian! Took a bullet in the crossfire!" says one of the soldiers, panting. A quick glance is enough to see that he's dead. I cover the body. "Put the stretcher down there," says the doctor, pointing at a hedgerow.

I suddenly feel extremely thirsty, my throat dry like it would be at the end of a hard day's training. I look around for a source of water and spot a jerrycan in the cargo container of one of the Hummers. I yank it off the metal shelf which usually keeps it in position while the car's in motion and tilt the plastic container, crouching to take a sip from the little trickle. As I'm drinking, one of the guys, a young trainee soldier with a thin face, walks over to me looking pale.

"I think there's someone in the bushes," he whispers.

"What do you—*someone?*" I can't keep quiet. "We're surrounded by terrorists!" I grab my weapon, almost knocking over the jerrycan on the spot. "We arrest him or shoot him!" I bark. "Guys, there's someone in the bushes!" I shout, crouching behind a mound nearby.

I strain my eyes, trying to see through the tangled branches where the soldier saw the mysterious figure lurking.

"Outflank him from there," I say, signaling to three soldiers to encircle the mound. Feldman and I move ahead cautiously. I think I see someone on the ground, a short distance away from the bush. I feel fear spreading throughout my body. Someone has been watching us all this time, waiting for the right moment to massacre us in a hail of bullets. Just like the pile of bodies of Kibbutz Nachal Oz residents we saw a short while ago, sprawled on the grass.

"*Waqf!*" I shout in Arabic — *Stop!* — in the most threatening tone I can muster. "*Arfae yaðayk!*" Hands in the air!

"It's a man! Hiding behind the hay!" shout the three soldiers on the outside flank.

Adrenaline froths through my body. The other soldiers join in the shouting. I keep moving forward. I can see him now clearly. "*Tahal lehon! Arfae yaðayk, walak ana batukhak!*" Raise your hands or I'll shoot!

He comes out toward us. He looks frightened. His clothes are tattered and drenched in blood, but he isn't injured. I feel a great urge to shoot him.

"Tie him up!" I tell one of the soldiers, while Feldman holds his gun to his head. He knocks the terrorist to the ground and cuffs his hands with a cable tie. The young soldier with the skinny face handles the terrorist gently, as if asking him for permission to tie him up. "For the love of God, what's wrong with you?" I snap at him, losing it. "Do you realize this jihadist might have slaughtered civilians here a couple of hours ago? Tie up his legs. Blindfold him. Tie his head to the car if you can!"

We cuff the detainee to the chassis of one of the Hummers, and I continue barking instructions at the soldier. I can't get the sight of the bodies strewn across the lawn out of my head. It's like a computer screensaver burned into my retinas.

"From now on, till further notice, you're going to aim your weapon at his head. If he tries to resist, you shoot him, got it?" I snarl, and the thin-faced soldier nods. He gets down on one knee, pressing the barrel of his gun to the terrorist's head. I step away and take a deep breath, trying to collect my senses. *Guy, why are you so angry?* This sweet young man—he must be eighteen, nineteen—is probably fresh out of basic training. He was called back from his home in the middle of a holiday and sent straight into this carnage.

I remember that I haven't had anything to drink yet and walk over to fill my empty water bottles from the jerry-cans, passing them around to the team. I insist that everyone else have a drink too. I rummage through my medical kit, checking what I still have left after treating Amichai. While counting how many infusion needles I've still got, I hear the sound of an engine. It's Hercules, back from his mission. He parks the car and leaps out of the driver's seat, yanking off his protective goggles and helmet.

"Did you deliver the package alive?" I ask him warily.

"I drove till I saw an ambulance heading my way in the other direction, and I honked to make it stop. We nearly crashed but I gave them Amichai." A look of satisfaction appears on his face. I pat him on the shoulder.

"Guy, can you come here a sec?" asks the thin-faced soldier. He points to the terrorist's cuffed feet. "They're really blue, they're not getting any blood. Do you think

I can loosen his restraints?" he says anxiously. Anxious because of me — not the terrorist.

I can feel a roar rising in my throat, a fiery speech coming together in my head. I'm about to eviscerate him. *Oh, the terrorist is uncomfortable? His feet aren't getting enough blood? Well, the whole damn kibbutz is covered in bodies, the son of a bitch can sniff the bloodstains on his shirt and try to work out which blot belongs to which body, so as far as I'm —*

I catch myself before opening my mouth. The soldier's eyes grab my attention. He's kneeling next to the terrorist, while I stand above him. Through his glasses, with their Coke bottle lenses, I see a deep expression of empathy and pity. I groan, resigned. "Just make sure someone else points his gun at him while you're loosening the cable ties." He nods and calls Hercules to help him.

The voice of the company commander, who's still leading his teams through the kibbutz, crackles over the radio: "*I want the 669 guys back inside on the Front line.*"

"Roger. Heading back," says Feldman.

We go back to the kibbutz, into the same apocalyptic hellscape for a second time. And the second time, the scene penetrates much deeper. Initially, the shock and fear stopped the information from reaching our brains. We walk fast, my heart pumping quickly. We link up with the guys still operating inside, now closing in on another neighborhood that still hasn't been swept.

Along with one of the company's squads, we cling to the outside wall of one of the buildings, and by shouting to the family hiding inside, we make sure that the house is clear. Bullet holes adorn the wall of the building, like specks of gray rice. We go inside — no need to open the door as it's already been blown off its hinges. The interior of the living room is dim. The power's been cut off; broken windowpanes and shards of glass are sprayed across the floorboards. I wonder to myself whether the Hamas attack included taking down vital infrastructure. There's no signal and no electricity. At this point, I realize anything is possible.

"I need a paramedic!" yelps a voice outside.

I search for the voice's owner, running around the building, and reach what looks like a side door leading to a utility room.

"Is he alive? Can he be saved?" one of the soldiers asks me. A man wearing jeans and a black polo shirt is lying motionless on the smooth cement floor. His eyes are wide open. I'm pretty sure it's a dead body, but to be safe, I give him a quick check. "Nothing we could do here," I say. For someone who's never seen a dead body before, like the soldier who called me over, the sight of someone sprawled on the floor like that is pretty unnerving. He tries to look away, doing his best not to make eye contact with the lifeless pupils.

Suddenly, I notice the strong smell of cooking gas.

I look around. I see two cylinders of cooking gas, latched onto the adjacent wall. "Try to stop the leak from the cylinders," I ask the soldier, trying to keep him occupied with something else, so he won't keep staring at the body.

What a naive baby I was, thinking it was a leak...

I head back into the building and pour myself a cup of water from the faucet in the dark kitchen. There's a frying pan on the stove, still gleaming with oil, and a small pot with leftover rice. I hear a girl sobbing in the corridor, try to track down the sound, and trace it to the family's safe room. Sitting in the dark, on the fold-out sofa bed, is a woman and a few children. Despite the thick darkness, it's clear the woman is exhausted. I crouch, propping myself on my heels. I settle down at the kids' eye level, light a small flashlight, and smile.

"Hi, I'm Guy. I'm a paramedic. Is everyone okay?"

The woman answers, "We're simply exhausted. We've been hiding here for hours. In the morning, the terrorists tried to breach the door. And since then, I've been hiding here with my kids," she says, lifting one of the children, who starts crying.

I check the kids one by one. Ask them a few questions. As part of my fourth year of med school, I just finished an internship in the pediatric department. So I feel comfortable being around little kids. "How old is he?" I ask the woman.

"Three years and four months."

I extend my hand, leaving it dangling in the air, waiting for him. Eventually, he finds the courage and gives me a high-five. I pull a face, pretending to be hurt in the torchlight. "Woah, you're so strong!" The kid giggles and buries his head back in his mother's shoulder.

"Is there anyone else at home?" I ask the mother again. "Are there neighbors in the houses next door who need help?"

"I don't know. I have no idea what's going on. As soon as we heard about the attack, with the initial reports about terrorists, my husband went out to defend the kibbutzim, to fight the terrorists. I've been telling him for years that I'm fed up living here. Every few months, every time Hamas decides to shoot at Israel, we sleep in the safe room for weeks on end. The kids have grown up under rocket sirens," she says wearily. "But that's that. It's the last time. I swear. This time, we're moving. He loves it here, but this time I won't give in. As soon as he gets back home, we're moving."

Suddenly the pieces come together in my mind.

"What does your husband look like?" I ask her, trying to make my question sound like a casual aside. I'm hoping the flashlight is gloomy enough that she can't see the shifting expression on my face. She describes him, stroking her son's head. "Gotcha. Okay. We're here, if you need anything. We'll make sure to get you out of the kibbutz safely," I say. I add, as if asking a favor, "And can we get a sheet or a blanket of some sort, some old fabric you don't need anymore?"

"Sure. What do you need it for?" she asks, pulling a pink woolly sheet off a shelf in the closet in the room next door.

"To clean my rifle," I say in an even tone.

This isn't the time to tell her that her husband will never get a chance to leave Nachal Oz.

TAKE THE LEAD

October 7th, 2023
16:00
Guy
The entrance of Kfar Aza

Having managed to generally liberate the neighborhoods of Kibbutz Nachal Oz, we'd received another order: to head for a nearby town called Kfar Aza. Nothing, including the chaos at Nachal Oz, could have prepared us for what we'd be dealing with there.

We're at the entrance to the town, getting our bearings, when a muddy army cargo truck emerges, coming to a halt just in front of us. The heavy metal doors of the truck open, pulled apart with a powerful yank. "Three casualties!" someone shouts from the pitch-black space.

"Hold up, hold up!" I shout, trying to calm everyone down. "What's their condition?" I ask, directing my question to the disembodied voice from within the vehicle.

Its owner emerges and comes over to me, his sweaty face mere inches from my face. "Dude, I'm begging you. We need more medical kits. I'm out of tourniquets!" he shouts.

"I don't have any. I'm sorry," I answer, tears of frustration in my eyes. "I swear I'm trying to get more too, I'm fresh out." The same medic had already asked me the same thing the last few times he'd brought casualties my way. "I wish I had something." I tap my pockets and tactical vest, as if to prove that I'm telling the truth—almost as if he asked me for a cigarette, not life-saving equipment for critically wounded soldiers.

Feldman and Dan haul out the casualties from the floor of the army cargo truck—which is pretty much the furthest thing from an ambulance or medical evacuation vehicle. "Help me get them down onto the stretchers," I order two soldiers, who are wafting around like ghosts, visibly in shock. I point to the open stretchers lying on the sidewalk by the side of the road to make sure they've caught my drift.

Another casualty lowers himself out of the truck. His face is contorted with pain, his arm gushing with blood, a tourniquet fastened tightly just below the shoulder. I look behind me, praying to see a car speeding our way down the road, but to no avail. So I only have one vehicle for evacuation. None of the others are back from the helipad yet, which is where I sent the previous batch of casualties. I'm guessing it'll be at least twenty minutes before they're back—and that's assuming the helicopters actually made it.

I crouch down, examining the casualties' condition up close. One of them is unconscious. Immobile. His eyes are closed, and I notice a bullet hole through his shoulder, through which blood is still gushing out. He's in a really bad state, and deathly pale. The second casualty is semi-conscious and muttering to himself. He has multiple wounds in his abdomen, either from bullets or shrapnel—it's hard to tell.

"Okay, get the seriously injured one into an ambulance!" someone shouts, taking hold of the handles of the stretcher carrying the unconscious casualty with the shoulder wound. Other soldiers run over to help him.

"No one move! Wait for my instructions," I bark, freezing them in place. The greater the chaos, the clearer you have to be about who's in charge. And this isn't just chaos—it's an absolute dumpster fire.

The thing is, my own decision-making is sluggish too; I'm distracted by all the thoughts whirling through my head. Our vehicle is an ambulance that belongs to United Hatzalah, a civilian EMS organization staffed by dedicated volunteers, but it's definitely not a military ambulance, which would be way better equipped for treating trauma injuries. Both my casualties are in critical condition. Both need urgent care and evacuation to an operating room. But there's no way to get both onboard. I need to make a snap decision about which one gets our medical resources. "Decision" is actually a fancy way of saying something much harsher. I need to choose who I give a chance to live and who will likely die on the side of the road.

"Load the one with the abdomen injury on to the ambulance," I say quietly. Against my instincts, I choose the casualty I believe, or at least hope, has the best chance of surviving, and not the more seriously injured one, who's profusely bleeding right in front of me. "Help the guy with the tourniquet get in the front seat. He can be evacuated sitting up."

In a second, the stretcher is raised in the air and thrust through the back doors of the ambulance. "Oxygen, monitoring, and fluid infusion according to trauma protocol!" I shout to the Hatzalah volunteer medic. The engine is already running. The driver jumps into his seat, and they speed off toward the main road. That casualty needs intensive treatment from a doctor or a paramedic; a blood transfusion, advanced monitoring, and maybe even resuscitation. But for now, none of that is relevant. We don't have any of those things on hand.

I turn my attention to the second casualty. "Bring me medical equipment, anything, whatever's left," I mumble, sitting down on the cold sidewalk, next to the young man's head. I place my fingers on his neck, trying to get a sense of his condition. His face is battered and he's unconscious. There are indications of shrapnel wounds around his chest. He's barely breathing and his shoulder is bleeding relentlessly, despite one of the soldiers applying pressure to the wound. There's no way to apply a tourniquet to a shoulder. If I had to put a medical diagnosis in writing, I would write: *goner.*

"Keep pressing, as hard as you can!" I tell the soldier.

"Hand me a cric kit[12] and needles to drain the chest," I tell Dan. He quickly assembles the kit. I massage the man's ribs, find the right spot, and stick the needle through his skin and muscle. Then, I do the same with another needle on the other side of his chest. If he's struggling to breathe because of a chest injury, this will improve his condition—but I don't have the chance to check. We hear gunfire, somewhere not too far away, like a warning barrage that the next casualties are on their way. Dan hands me a scalpel and I start cutting at the bottom of the casualty's throat, exposing his windpipe and shoving a plastic pipe inside. I connect the bag and start ventilating him, squeezing the rubber valve, pumping air into his lungs.

---

12 A cricothyrotomy is an infrequent procedure that involves placement of a tube through an incision in the cricothyroid membrane to establish an airway for oxygenation and ventilation.

I raise my head. Praying that maybe, by some miracle, one of the ambulances is back from the helipad already. But the junction is empty. *We are so screwed.*

"Where's Shmuel?" I ask, looking for one of the Hatzalah volunteers. Soon after arriving, I'd picked out Shmuel; he was a particularly assertive volunteer, and the others listened to him. I'd appointed him as ad hoc commander of Hatzalah forces at the scene; for the last few hours, he's been my right-hand man.

"Guy, I'm here. What do you need?" he says, reporting for duty.

I can't believe I'm about to do this.

"You!" I say, pointing to the soldier using a bandage to apply pressure to the bleeding shoulder. "Your entire role in the world is to put pressure on that shoulder. Try to stop the bleeding." He nods, his hands already shaking — either from exhaustion or from the importance of his task. "And you," I say, grabbing another soldier by the sleeve, "pump this valve every five seconds." He nods.

I signal for the others to lift the stretcher and point to a civilian car parked by the side of the road: a pickup truck with an open cargo bed. We might have to lay down the stretcher on a pile of work tools or vegetable crates.

"Shmuel, get someone behind the wheel. Full speed till the helipad." The stretcher carrying the casualty is lifted into the cargo bed, spilling fresh blood everywhere. The pickup truck sets off for the road with the medical team: two soldiers who've probably never seen a casualty like this in real life. I watch them speed off till the car shrinks to a blurry fleck on the horizon and disappears.

I'm left alone with my thoughts. That soldier went to battle and fought to free hostages who'd been trapped as human shields by their savage captors — in their own homes. He deserved so much more. At the very least, he deserved for us to have been there for him, and to have received the best medical care possible. He definitely didn't deserve what he actually got.

He looks like he's Ari's age, at most. *Ari*. The fleeting thought of my little brother fills me with horror, like an electric current racing up my spine. I try to block out the mental image of him in uniform, at the head of a company under fire. I'm struggling to keep that terrible image from searing itself into my brain. I pray that Ari isn't in danger right now, that he's not engaged in face-to-face combat with terrorists—and, if he is, I really hope that the medical teams are nearby, as they're supposed to be, and that they're doing their best to treat casualties at the scene.

But that unconscious warrior who took a bullet to the shoulder—who fought valiantly to rescue civilians —should have received an appropriate level of care. We should have been prepared and equipped for this catastrophic scenario. He deserved the highest standard of medical attention, with the best resources that the army could offer. Yet, in his moment of need, we gave him absolutely nothing even close to that.

By now we've been at Kibbutz Kfar Aza for a few hours. When we arrived, Dan parked the Toyota in a gravelly area about thirty yards from the yellow gate. Finally, the cell reception came back. My parents had sent numerous worried messages directly to me and in the family group chat, asking how I was doing. I also received one from Noga:

> *"I'm on my way south. Let me know what's happening with you."*

Shit. Why isn't she staying on base?

I try calling Ari again. His phone doesn't even ring.

I try to suppress the image of Noga in a convoy of open-topped vehicles, bounced up and down in the back of a Hummer, going past intersections where barely an hour earlier, jihadists had ambushed IDF forces. *Guy, focus. She's okay.*

Trust her.

The first thing we did upon arrival is link up with the deputy commander of 669, Ben. He's the one who told us to come here and, apparently, he had arrived with another rescue soldier moments before us.

The three of us hop off our pickup truck and approach him.

"Hey guys," Ben says. We're gathered around him on the curb of the access road, waiting to receive our mission. I gather that a Hamas squad has managed to infiltrate the kibbutz; I assume he has some details about the incident and our mission ahead—like any other of the dozens of rescue missions I'd been part of before.

"Look," he says, "IDF forces that entered the kibbutz ran into an ambush, there are now—"

Suddenly, we hear frantic shouting from the direction of the entrance gate. I see an APC speeding toward us from the other side of the gateway, approaching a group of soldiers standing on the road. One of them frantically starts signaling to the APC, trying to slow it, but it's too late, and it slams into an army vehicle parked across the road. I see it happen in slow-motion, like in a movie.

"We've got casualties!" someone shouts.

Several casualties, actually, with gunshot wounds. I help load them onto stretchers and into vehicles. It's complete mayhem. Everyone's shouting at everyone else, and it's unclear who is supposed to evacuate the injured—or who's even responsible for treating them, for that matter. I try to work out who's even commanding this scene.

After several long minutes—way longer than it should have taken—the casualties are finally transported away, disappearing down the road in a cloud of dust. We circle back to Ben, who's speaking on the phone, apparently trying to understand where the helicopters can land. He hangs up.

"Is there a person in charge of the situation here?" I ask, looking around. There's a gaggle of people milling around us. Some wearing uniforms, others in civilian clothes, all armed. In all, there are ten, maybe twenty people.

My question hangs in the air for the duration of an awkward pause. Then Ben replies, hesitantly.

"Don't think so."

"Okay, so what do we do now?" I ask.

Ben pauses for a moment. "Try to work out where you'll be most useful and take the lead," he says.

And then, from nowhere, there's gunfire all around us. Instinctively, I thump the magazine in my rifle to double-check it's in right. The cogs in my mind are spinning rapidly. I've never been thrown into an operation and just told: *make your own mission, just take initiative.* I exchange some words with Dan and Feldman. We're all still hoping that someone will come up to us with an orderly briefing of the battle plan, that someone will tell us what to do. After all, we're just reservists. I'm a medical student, for God's sake. I'm not a senior officer just a paramedic who's suddenly found himself here.

We try to put together a plan for how to enter the kibbutz and extract casualties. I'm still half-expecting someone to run up and tell us, *Guys, I need you here, there, treat him, save her, help them, bring that*—anything. But nobody says a word. Nobody asks us for anything. The realization starts to settle in: we're on our own out here.

I hear a burst of gunfire nearby, and it sets off a firestorm of shooting from all sides. The gunshots reverberate everywhere, as if the whole kibbutz were under a blizzard of bullets.

DON'T LOOK

October 7th, 2023
18:00
Winnick
Flying west from Israel's south toward
the Gaza Envelope

While I'm trying to come up with a plan outside Kfar Aza, Winnick and his team are flying west from Be'er-Sheva in their helicopter—the fourth time they've been called out to the next mission from the Medical Center.

"Reports of an attack on a base near Gaza border. Multiple casualties. Looks like we'll land just outside the post and enter on foot." Barnea conveys to the team standing around him the details he just received over the radio system. He places a firm hand on the doctor's shoulders. "I need you to get a quick impression of the casualties' conditions, and we'll take them to the hospital." And then he refers to the rest of the team. "We are about to land. Grab your weapons, and be ready to disembark." The doctor and the rest of the team at the front of the Sikorsky CH-53 Sea Stallion helicopter nod, signaling that they heard him.

"T-minus two," the pilot updates them. The team members haul their bags on their backs and hang their rifles around their necks, ready to dart out of the chopper. Winnick stands next to Barnea and leans on the helicopter wall in order to keep his balance when they land. He performs a quick audio check, making sure he can hear the pilots on the agreed radio frequency through his headset. His role on the team is to be Barnea's right-hand man. He feels the helicopter tilting to one side, making one final turn above ground before landing. The mechanic's head pokes out through the ramp, the back hatch of the helicopter, checking there are no obstacles, especially rocks, that might crunch into the belly of the chopper or hit the tail rotor as they land.

The tires hit the ground, the mechanic opens the ramp, and the team sails out into a cloud of dust, dry vegetation flying in every direction.

They run along the sandy path down to the gate of the military post. To their left are movable concrete walls, creating a mighty wall protecting the post from gunfire from the nearby Gaza Strip. Around them are fields and groves belonging to one of the neighboring kibbutzim. "Hannah," Barnea calls the doctor, "if there's a paramedic at the post, take details from him about—" He stops mid-sentence. His feet stop in sync. In front of them, right next to the big metal gate, are elongated human shadows. Three Hamas gunmen's bodies are lying on the asphalt, still wearing tactical vests full of ammunition. Barnea skirts around them, instinctively pointing his weapon at the corpses of the terrorists.

"What's going on here...?" Barnea mumbles.

"IDF! IDF!" shouts Winnick as they storm the gate, wondering how big the battle was that very recently raged inside. The wall along the gate has been breached, and two people could easily wriggle through the opening in the concrete. A secondary gate next to the main gate was also breached. "Looks like terrorists raided the post," he mutters, totally unprepared for the sight that welcomed them upon landing.

In the narrow sandy forecourt of the outpost roughly the size of a basketball court, there are two military vehicles on fire. A dozen casualties are lying around, most sprawled on the floor, some on stretchers. Some of those on the ground appear to be dead, lying motionless.

"Where's 669? Can I get a medic? Any sort of doctor? I need help!" someone shouts at them. Winnick spots soldiers' bodies at the entrance to what looks like the dining hall, because at the entrance to the prefab building is a bowl with pitchers for Jewish ritual handwashing before meals.

They start to sift through the casualties and apply first aid.

Barnea radios the pilots to report, "There are more than ten casualties here. I need to be on the ground for a few minutes at least."

Meanwhile, Winnick walks over to the group of soldiers standing near the vehicles, or at least, near what is left of them. The smell of burned plastic floods the air. "What about you guys?" he asks them. Four soldiers, all smoking a cigarette. One of them responds with a blank stare like a bored schoolkid. Completely mute, his eyes are full of tears. The others continue smoking, as if they didn't hear him. "Are you okay? Are any of you injured?" Winnick asks.

The soldier with the blank expression shakes his head. The others still ignore him. Winnick wonders whether to try and put them to work, to help carry the stretchers and treat their wounded comrades. Not only because it wouldn't hurt to have extra helping hands in a mass-casualty incident, but also because it would help treat their shell shock. *So that's what it looks like*, he thinks to himself. *Exactly how they described battle shock to us back in the unit's medics' course.*

"Winnick, where are you?" he hears Barnea calling him. He walks over to him. "I've got the company commander here," Barnea says, gesturing at the officer next to him. "He says you can land the chopper here in the middle of the base." Winnick looks around, examining the terrain, but doesn't think it is possible. There is not enough space between the row of cars and the dining hall. Barnea sees that Winnick looks skeptical and decides that they should check the option anyway. "Speak with the pilots, check if it's possible," he orders Winnick and goes back to helping prepare the casualties for evacuation.

"Eagle, it's Wildcats, do you copy?" Winnick radios the pilots circling overhead, waiting from a distance.

"Loud and clear, what's the situation?" one of them answers.

"Do you think you can land inside the post?" asks Winnick.

"Give me a second."

Winnick hears a whirring sound rapidly approaching. The helicopter is flying in a circle, pivoting to one side, so the pilots can get a better view of the site from the cockpit. "What the hell is going on?" mutters one of the pilots under his breath, taking in the destruction and casualties lying all over the place. A few seconds later, they give Winnick their final answer. "Negative, we can't do it. The site's too small, and anyway, there are electrical cables obstructing the descent," says the pilot. "We'll have to meet you outside." The disappointment in his voice is crystal clear, even over the radio. They're powerless to help.

Suddenly, one of the smoking soldiers walks over to Winnick. "Bro, you hear me? There are more casualties in the kitchen," he says quietly, pointing at the canteen. "That's the back section of the dining hall."

Winnick nods and trots over to the gloomy building. The power has been cut off to the whole site. The flashlight on his helmet points a ray of light at the dark building, a one-story prefab structure with a covered concrete enclosure outside the front door. Winnick wonders whether to go back and update Barnea but decides that it would be a waste of time. If there are casualties there, he will bring them over quickly. He stands next to the entrance for a second. The stench of bleach and chicken soup powder welcomes him in. His heart is pounding. Stepping away from the chaos of the casualties outside, he begins to clock that it will take him time to understand the magnitude of the disaster here.

Suddenly, he spots a flashing light from a nearby trailer that looks like a dormitory for the base's soldiers. He raises his rifle to chest level, ready to shoot. Slowly, he inches forward. His gun cocked, his finger up, next to the trigger. He presses himself against the dusty white paneled wall of the prefab and walks up to the window, steadily lifting his head to the metal frame to peek inside.

The source of the flashing light becomes clear in an instant. A mirror hanging on the wall, next to a bunk bed. But he will never forget the scene around the bed. On the floor lies the body of a soldier—his head cut off, completely severed from his torso. His uniform is one big puddle of blood. On a bed in front of the door is another soldier. His uniform is shredded, and his body is covered in deep gashes, knife wounds. His head is limply hanging off the metal frame of the bed, eyes wide open.

The scene hits him like a punch to the gut. Winnick can't take his eyes off it for several seconds. His thoughts freeze and he loses all sense of time. Feeling like he is bound up in heavy chains, he takes a deep breath. Chills spread through his body like an electric current, refusing to dissipate. Suddenly, he remembers why he came here in the first place. There is a casualty in the kitchen. *Snap out of it*, he tells himself. *Close your eyes and step away from the window.*

Winnick speeds back over to the dining hall, forcing what he saw to the back of his mind. He steps into the gloomy canteen; long tables are covered in festive white tablecloths, and a cardboard box with challahs for Shabbat is sitting on a nearby table. Plastic chairs are all over the place. Winnick feels fear spreading through his bones. He shines his flashlight from side to side, trying to detect any movement. "Anyone here?" he shouts into the darkness. A strong whiff of meat stew hangs heavy in the air, but apart from the food that has been slow-cooking since Friday morning, there's another smell. The powerful smell of cooking gas.

"Hello? Anyone?" shouts Winnick again, struggling to breathe. The pungent smell of gas grabs him by the throat. He inches toward the opening behind the serving counters, long tables with rectangular holes for keeping dishes warm during mealtime. He edges through the doorway and into the adjacent building, serving as the kitchen. As soon as he steps in, he can no longer breathe. It's like stepping into a pool of gas. He leaps back with a prickly cough. It feels like someone blocked off his windpipe in an instant. Struggling to catch his breath, he feels an urgent need to throw up.

Winnick checks his watch. He has been dallying for too long. He assumes Barnea is already looking for him, wondering where he's gone. Winnick takes another look at the dark doorway, staring it down like an enemy standing between him and his mission. A thought pops into his mind: *retreat*. He understands it's dangerous. The smell of gas is so strong that for a moment, he thinks the air has changed color. He understands that if he takes a single breath of air in that rancid kitchen, the gas might make his lungs explode. On the other hand, he can't stop thinking about the casualty inside, the thought screaming in his mind. It's like there's someone calling him.

He makes his decision. Winnick fills his lungs with air. *In out, in out*, several times. Breathing deeply and exhaling sharply. He closes his eyes for a moment, trying to concentrate, to slow down his pulse, like he knows from maritime rescue drills, when the wind from the rotor pulsating above him out at sea creates waves that crash onto his head and risk drowning him, and he's got to keep calm and in control. Winnick takes one big final breath, fills his lungs to their maximum capacity, feels his ribs expanding like a balloon inside his tactical vest, and breaks into a run toward the kitchen.

His headlamp illuminates a wide stainless steel table in the middle of the room. Next to the wall are two sinks as large as bathtubs. He walks around the table, the insufferable stench stinging and burning his nostrils—a hint of what is to come if he dares to take a breath. *You've got loads of oxygen, loads of oxygen*, he tells himself on a loop, like a reassuring mantra. He continues into the adjacent room. Piles of boxes of pasta and rice are next to long shelves packed with cans and tins. On the far side of the room is an industrial kitchen, and next to it, an opening that seems to lead to another room. *How big is this place?* It's a kitchen that's supposed to serve the needs of a tiny military post. If Hamas had decided to besiege the post instead of raiding it, they would have been just fine.

Winnick's head begins to spin. He wonders whether it's the gas or the lack of oxygen—or both. He feels his diaphragm shaking, a natural bodily impulse to shout to the brain: out of air! *Just this one room, just one quick look, and I'm out of here*, he tells himself. He walks through the doorway between the rooms. He leans slightly forward, planning just to take a peek and not go in. He hears Barnea's voice in his radio headset, informing him that the rest of the team is starting to evacuate the casualties, asking the chopper to land as close as possible.

Then, he sees her. In the middle of the room, between the metal dishes and pots, lies a female soldier wearing a uniform, her weapon cast aside. Winnick's muscles are screaming for oxygen already. He grabs her limp shoulders and takes big strides backward, dragging her along the length of the room. His eyes feel like they are about to explode. Incredible pressure is building up in his forehead. His whole body is crying out for air. *Don't breathe! Don't breathe!* he tells himself, gripping her with his last ounces of strength. Her head sways between his arms. *Just a little further…* He feels his legs failing him. He crashes into the large steel table, sending a chopping board flying to the ground. *You've got loads of oxygen, loads of oxygen.* He can feel his heartbeat thumping intensely, practically echoing in his brain.

He barely makes it across the threshold of the building. Winnick's body fails and his head hits the serving counter. His breathing reflex gets the better of him and he takes a huge breath of air, gasping desperately for oxygen. He feels like he's being stabbed in the chest. He leans forward, resting his hands on his knees, trying to catch his breath. His head spins like crazy. *This isn't over, you've got to keep going*, he tells himself. The soldier's green eyes stare at him. He places a hand on her neck. No pulse. A red hole in the center of her chest. Her face is gray. The thought of leaving her here passes through his mind for a split-second but goes as quickly as it came. He lies down on the soldier's abdomen, and with a quick roll, hoists her up on his shoulders and strides out of the canteen. Even with the soldier's full bodyweight pressing on his neck, the air outside, still reeking of smoke, feels like pure oxygen to him. He walks quickly over to the stretchers at the gates of the base.

Hannah, the doctor, sees Winnick coming. "What's the casualty's condition?" she shouts. Winnick doesn't answer. He lays the soldier down on the ground next to Hannah. He clings to the faintest doubt, the slightest chance that it might still be possible to do something. Hannah walks over and, in a matter of seconds, declares the case closed with a shake of her head, her lips pursed.

Winnick spots a green sheet thrown by the curb, takes it, and covers the young woman's body with a gentle motion, from her feet up to her head—as if tucking her into bed.

"Let's go, pick up the stretchers!" barks Barnea. His team and the survivors of the attack on the base hoist the stretchers up in the air. Hannah pumps a manual resuscitator with her hand, sending oxygen into one casualty's lungs.

The soldiers head out for the open field. They pass by the gates—the breached side gate, and the new hole that Hamas blew open through the concrete wall. Winnick's lungs are still recovering, breathing rapidly as if he were climbing a mountain at high-altitude. A stretcher pole is propped on his shoulder. He observes the stretcher in front of them, his headlight on, suddenly lighting up the terrorists' bodies. He looks away immediately. The casualties bouncing up and down on the stretchers groan in agony as the gravel crunches underfoot. The sound of the

helicopter's rotors reverberates through the night's darkness, as the beast prepares to land in a nearby field.

"What's that over there in the bushes?" shouts Alex
suddenly. And before anyone can respond, they're hit with
enemy fire.

BREAK IT DOWN

October 7th, 2023
19:00
Guy
The entrance to Kfar Aza

"Can anyone here give treatment? A doctor, para-medic, medic?" I shout at the top of my lungs, standing in the middle of the main road leading to Kibbutz Kfar Aza. "Anyone with any level of training, or with any equipment—come to me right now!" I wait, Dan and Feldman by my side. I'm expecting at least ten people to run over. Even on flights, there's always a doctor on board. But it's two. Just two people. One of them was a medic in his mandatory service, twenty years ago. The other is a weekend volunteer medic with Magen David Adom.

I feel a chill down my spine. *Deep breaths.* The firefight inside the kibbutz goes on and on. It sounds like there's more than one terrorist cell—*but how many terrorists could possibly have infiltrated Israel?* I think to myself. Rockets and mortars are flying everywhere. This is absurd, borderline suicidal. It's just me and another four medics. No ambu-lances, no helicopter on the way to whisk us to safety. I feel a sense of helplessness spreading through my limbs, a crippling fear.

And suddenly, out of the front gate of the kibbutz, comes a fresh batch of casualties—and I accept the fact that we're alone. No one is coming to save us; or to lead us; or to rescue us.

The gunfire in the kibbutz rages on. Terrorists are clearly everywhere. Casualties keep pouring out non-stop, dozens or maybe hundreds already. There are soldiers with horrific gunshot wounds, as well as civilians who managed to survive the terrorist massacre but who are traumatized to the depths of their souls. I don't touch the corpses or casualties without a pulse. We lay them down on the edge of the row of trees between the sidewalk, which is doubling up as a makeshift hospital, and in a nearby grove—the same grove where the terrorist cell hid before opening fire minutes ago.

Amidst the carnage, I think back to when I was in paramedics' course, which I was sent to right after finishing the 669 pipeline. During an ambulance shift in Haifa, the paramedic leading my training once turned to me and said, "Guy, there's a widespread belief that the way to deal with a mass-casualty incident is to manage it. That's not right. You don't manage a mass-casualty incident. You break it down." We were talking just after dealing with four casualties from a car crash. That's what passes for a mass-casualty incident. He was definitely not trying to tell me what the rulebook says to do when you have dozens of casualties that keep flooding in with no end in sight. And I never could have imagined needing to know.

Even so, I stick to the basic premise he taught me. *Break it down.* Disperse the casualties. Send them in every possible direction to places that might have medical equipment. That's the first task. The second task—a mission I give myself—is to keep the one access road to the kibbutz clear for traffic. Forces have to get in; casualties have to get out. This narrow road is the only artery breathing life into Kfar Aza. I have to make sure it stays clear.

We're out of medical equipment. There are no ambulances, and no paramedics or doctors, either. The deputy commander of our unit had to run somewhere else. Alongside the reinforcements coming in, we also have some Hatzalah volunteers, wearing fluorescent orange vests—not exactly ideal clothing for a warzone crawling with hundreds of armed terrorists.

We were instructed over the radio to send casualties to various extraction sites nearby, but it's unclear if there are even enough helicopters reaching those places. It's completely possible that I'm sending dying soldiers and civilians off in the back of pickup trucks to random places in vain; there's no guarantee that anyone's coming to meet them there. I have no clue. I've been begging people over the phone, and over the comms systems, to speak with Unit 669, with the Medical Corps, with anyone who might have medical equipment or ambulances to send us. We ran out of equipment a while ago; the only treatment I can give now is using belts and strips of fabric, as if we're dealing with a medieval battle. Meanwhile, nothing is coming our way other than more injured people. I feel like everything around me is disintegrating. A mass-casualty incident, a battlefield, countless fatalities and injured, and it's all happening inside the territory of the country.

I watch the scene in despair, outwardly trying to maintain a serious, focused expression. I can't betray how drained to the core I feel. Then suddenly, the heavy growl of a vehicle speeding down the road penetrates the silence beyond the yellow gate. The car stops with a screech of the brakes. We open the doors. "Two casualties. Gunshot wounds to the limbs. Conscious," says a soldier in the car, hunched forward between the front seats. He looks familiar—he's already evacuated several casualties. I have no idea what unit he's from. All I know is that he's tall and has a pointed graying beard.

I reach out and help the casualties get out of the car. I check them over quickly and decide they can either be sent to the helipad sitting up in a civilian vehicle, or they'll have to wait for the next evacuation when the ambulances get back.

The soldier with the pointy beard leaps out of the car, revealing a pair of legs spread out on the floor. They have bloodstains and gashes all up and down. In a heartbeat, the soldier leans back inside where he was sitting with the casualties just a few seconds ago, and gives one of the mangled legs a sharp yank. The body flies several feet through the air and crashes onto the asphalt, emitting a terrible bellow of pain. Instinctively, I nearly scream at him in shock and fury: *what are you doing treating a casualty like that?!*

Then I see that the hands are cuffed. "Captured terrorist," the soldier adds quietly, before closing the back doors and hopping into the passenger's seat. They reverse and turn back into the kibbutz.

I'm left standing in the same spot, the bound terrorist feet away, trying to come to my senses. I feel pity and shock, the ultimate collision of compassionate empathy and primal rage. He's a terrorist, a bloodthirsty murderer who woke up in the morning to massacre civilians. A depraved enemy captured in battle, in innocent people's homes. I feel a whirlwind of emotions, an urge to treat and assist the helpless and injured human being lying in front of me, and at the same time, an intense desire to make him suffer.

"Get the captive out of here," I tell a group of soldiers. I push off any processing of my raging cognitive dissonance until later.

"Put him in the ditch." I point to the side of the road. "Double-check his cuffs and tie his legs," I add. A few minutes later, another car speeds our way, this time only with bound captives. They're not even injured. "Get them all in the ditch!" I shout. "Keep them as far away as possible from each other!"

This is now a whole new thing. I realize that our makeshift prison in the ditch needs some officers and some policies. *If just one of them is still armed, even with a single grenade,* I think to myself, *we're all goners.*

"I need someone who's free. Is there an officer here who can help with something?" I bark at the group of people huddling in the adjacent car park. The soldiers I randomly asked to assist me are having trouble guarding the captives, who keep piling up. They're having a hard time binding their legs.

"I'm free. What do you need?" says a tired-looking sergeant, walking up to me.

"Who are you, what are you doing here?" I ask him assertively. I'm thinking of the young man from Nachal Oz, the soldier who felt pangs of pity for the captive. A single captive is one thing, but with dozens of captives in the middle of an active war zone, I can't let anyone with a bleeding heart manage this ad hoc prison.

"I'm Elazar. I'm a platoon commander. My soldiers were injured. I evacuated them here. Ready for a task and fresh orders."

You're in.

I spot the cover on the sergeant's dog tag. It's from a Paratroopers' battalion. "The Paratroopers are the best. I did my basic training with the 890th Battalion, in

November '13," I say, trying to make a personal connection and inject some humanity into the pressure cooker we're both trapped inside. A smile spreads across his weary face.

"You've just received your fresh orders," I say, placing a hand on his shoulder. "You see that ditch?" I say, pointing at the roadside. He nods. "That's the ditch where I'm sending all the captives, the terrorists captured in combat. They've got to be tied up. And far from each other. Don't let any of them say a word. And frisk them, one by one, check that they don't have any ammo or ordinances on them. These are terrorists who came to murder innocent families, do you understand that?"

"Got it," he answers, accepting the mission I've just assigned him, by virtue of the extemporaneous authority I just vested in myself.

"Are you definitely up for it?"

"Yes," he says defiantly, as if trying to prove that he's fit for his new role as prison manager.

"Where's Guy?" someone shouts. "They're on the radio, they're saying more casualties!" I pat Elazar on the shoulder and turn to the APC speeding up the road.

HELP FROM THE HEAVENS

October 7th, 2023
20:30
Winnick
An army outpost by the Gaza border

While I'm trying to figure out a practical plan to evacuate the casualties from the kibbutz entrance, Barnea and Winnick have even bigger problems.

"Ambush!" shouts Barnea. "Take cover!"

Out of pure muscle memory, still there even years after basic training, Winnick drops the stretcher—or, more accurately, throws it on the ground—and flies behind a nearby rock, searching for the source of the gunfire.

"Spread out! Spread out!" shouts Barnea. "Can anyone see where it's coming from?"

The gunfire continues. Brief bursts, from a distance of a few dozen feet at most. "From the woods over there!" shouts one of the soldiers from the army outpost, pointing at a row of trees bordering the field.

"*Barnea, do you copy?*" asks the pilot over the radio, watching from above the events on the ground through his night vision goggles.

Barnea doesn't answer. He still can't see where the terrorists are hiding.

"Enemy behind the trees, return fire!" shouts Winnick, who spots the brief flashes from their gun barrels but can't quite get a clear view of the terrorists themselves. He releases several exploratory bursts of gunfire in the direction of the tree line, and notices that the other soldiers around him are firing wildly in every direction. It's an extremely dangerous situation: the risk of a friendly fire incident is high.

Meanwhile, the pilots keep trying. *"Barnea, what's your situation? Are there casualties? We're here for anything you need,"* the pilot says, audibly concerned.

Winnick's heart is thumping. He picks himself up a little and tries to get a better view of the scene. The casualties are completely exposed. He tries to find a way to drag the stretchers to cover nearby, but can't find anywhere to evacuate them to quickly or safely. There's no other option: they have to neutralize the enemy. Several soldiers from the company run to the edge of the perimeter wall, where they'll be able to get a better shot into the bushes.

"Barnea?" the pilot asks again.

"We're in combat. I'll update you," Barnea barks tersely into his radio.

"Moving to a better position!" shouts one of the soldiers with a Negev light machine gun. "Give me cover!" He sprints toward the nearest concrete block and kneels next to it, the barrel of his Negev pressed clean against the gray wall.

Barnea's mind races feverishly, trying to work out what to do.

They're in open terrain. If they try to lift the stretchers and run back into the base, they'll be sitting ducks for the terrorists. They can't just run for it, because they don't know where the enemy is, and Barnea doesn't have enough men to outflank them. And while he's trying to make up his mind, their ammo is running out. Fast.

Barnea knows they're at a clear disadvantage. He takes a quick look behind him and sees Hannah, the doctor, lying next to one of the casualties, giving him a blood transfusion.

"Barnea, you copy?" asks the pilot again.

"Still in contact, we're taking fire," Barnea says brusquely, having taken cover behind a mound of earth. *What is there to understand?? WE'RE BEING SHOT AT!?*

"I've brought reinforcements," the pilot chimes in over the radio.

"Hammer here at your service, how can I help?" suddenly crackles a new voice over the headset. Barnea turns his head, looking up. There's another dark shadow hovering over them. He adjusts the night vision goggles on his helmet to be sure that he's seeing straight, and his face breaks into a huge grin.

"Winnick, get on the radio and direct the attack helicopter!" shouts Barnea.

Winnick hits the button on his comms device. "Hammer, it's Wildcats. Can you see the sandy path with the soldiers?"

"Roger that."

"Can you see a row of tall trees between the field and the grove?"

"Copy that."

Winnick helps the pilots aboard the attack helicopter, armed with lethal weapons systems, to get the lay of the battlefield, understanding where the friendlies are located while targeting the terrorists hiding in the scrub.

In an instant, a high-frequency drumming noise erupts in the sky and the cannon at the front of the helicopter, like a massive fang, sprays hellfire at the terrorists from above.

"Nobody shoot!" shouts Barnea to his team. He wants to hear whether the gunfire continues from the direction of the enemy, or whether Hammer managed to neutralize them. But the only sound in the distance is the whizzing of the rotors and the engines of the two helicopters hovering overhead.

"Wildcats from Hammer, what's your status? I'm not seeing any movement among the trees," says the attack helicopter pilot.

"All good" replies Barnea, panting and running over to one of the stretchers, grabbing both poles by himself. "Just one question. Where do I get a gun like yours?"

"Always at your service," chuckles the attack helicopter pilot as the chopper flies off and disappears into the dark night sky.

I DON'T WANT HELP

October 7th, 2023
22:00
Guy
Kfar Aza

"He says they got the order this morning. The plan is to get more Nukhba[13] forces in…" I overhear the interrogators in plain clothes standing a good few feet away from me. He's relaying the details he just managed to squeeze out of one of the captives to someone on the other end of the phone.

"I understand. I'll try to check," he says, hangs up, and rushes back to the detainee pen, now under the command of Elazar the paratrooper. The interrogators arrived a short while ago. I don't know whether they're from the Shin Bet,[14] the Police, or the IDF. The paratroopers helped them dress the captives in white overalls, like the suits that medical staff used to wear back in the early days of COVID.

Several figures are now covered in white hoods, their hands cuffed. Elazar's team is keeping watch over them — or, more accurately, guarding everyone else from the ter-

---

13   The commando unit of Hamas's terrorist forces.
14   The Israeli equivalent of the FBI.

rorists. Two interrogators arrived less than an hour ago to assess the threat. They're questioning the detained terrorists methodically, in fluent Arabic. Interchanging between cajoling and shouting, they glean information from the detainees about where the next attacks are planned for. I manage to catch fragments of the captured terrorists' sentences. Names, places, curse words.

"What are you doing?!" I suddenly hear someone shouting from the direction of the ditch. "Get the fuck away from him now!"

I turn around, looking for the source of the shouting, and immediately see a soldier kicking one of the terrorists, kicking him again and again like a punching bag. "You son of a bitch! You murdered him! I'm gonna kill you!" the soldier yells, his voice cracking. He keeps thrashing him, manically possessed. The captured terrorist is wailing. One of the interrogators forcefully pushes the soldier away, sending him crashing to the ground with a thud.

"He murdered my friends!" the soldier screams at the investigator. His voice is completely broken; it quickly morphs from enraged screams to muffled sobs.

Elazar runs over, helps the soldier back up, and quietly leads him out of the ditch. He sits him down on a rock, where he buries his head in his hands. In the darkness, I can see his shoulders quivering as he sits alone and weeps.

"Nobody touches any of the detainees!" one of the interrogators roars, pure fury in his eyes. "We are human beings, first and foremost, not animals! And we, our country, are under attack. Hamas invaded Israel. The next one to lift a finger against a detainee will have a personal score to settle with me! Is that clear?!" His voice echoes through the darkness. The investigator heads back over the trees, not far from where we placed the bodies.

It's almost midnight. We've just finished loading casualties into vehicles, but as we've been told that terrorists are still potentially lying in ambush at the road junctions, our instructions are that every vehicle evacuating casualties must be accompanied by an armed soldier. Feldman left half an hour ago and isn't back yet. And now Dan has gone with another ambulance to a nearby site, where we were told the helicopters would land. My throat is parched. Taking advantage of the short break, I look for some water. Judging by the sound of gunfire both near and far, I assume that it's only a matter of time until we receive fresh casualties.

Our original trio—Feldman, Dan, and I—has been joined by Smith and Cohen, two old teammates of mine, from Cohort 42. I have no idea how they got here—frankly, I haven't had a chance to ask them—but it's hard to overstate how happy I am to have the two of them next to me.

"Guy, we have casualties!" announces Smith, seeing a military vehicle speeding our way. My body tenses up. I'm focusing on the vehicle careening toward us, getting ready to work quickly and efficiently. I look behind me. The ambulances aren't back yet from the helipad, which means more improvising.

The vehicle stops with a screech of the brakes and the driver leaps out. "Civilians, they're not injured. They're okay," he says.

A woman and four children step out of the car. Suddenly, we hear shouting in Arabic from behind the trees, where the interrogators are questioning the detainees. I notice the alarm in the eyes of one of the kids, gripping the woman's hand for dear life.

"Everything's okay. They're IDF troops. They're speaking Arabic," I quip, trying to sound casual. I'm trying to reassure civilians who have just been rescued from the kibbutz, from the safe rooms of their homes. They can't be allowed to stay here. We'll be receiving fresh casualties any minute, and the children can't be allowed to see them. I also realize, from the way the children are behaving, that my attempt to explain away the shouting in Arabic hasn't helped to calm their nerves. They understand that these are the terrorists who burned their community to the ground using the cooking gas tanks connected to the house's kitchen. But where am I meant to send them? Why the hell isn't there a bus here, waiting to pick up the locals and take them out of harm's way? Who's even in charge of evacuating civilians in a situation like this anyway?

"Elazar!" I holler at the platoon commander-turned-prison manager, signaling for him to come over. "I need you to find me two available soldiers. I've got a task for them." In spurts, more IDF forces have been arriving at the scene. There are military vehicles parked in a nearby lot, but it looks like many of the troops are awaiting orders—waiting for someone to tell them what to do.

Elazar doesn't ask any questions. He calls over two of his subordinates. I skip the niceties and introductions. "Listen," I tell them, "more and more civilians are arriving. Anyone who isn't injured and doesn't need medical treatment has to be taken somewhere safe. That's what I need you to do." The two men nod, waiting for me to tell them where this "safe place" is. I pause for a second and look around. I see a bus standing at a nearby gas station, on the other side of the dirt parking lot that's rapidly filling up with military vehicles.

"Do you see that bus there?" I say, pointing at it. "That bus is for evacuating civilians." It's a decision I've made on the spot, giving this bus a whole new identity. I have no idea who the bus belongs to, or whether the driver is even there. Maybe he was killed, maybe he fled, maybe he's lying injured somewhere in the bushes. But until I have a better solution, I'd rather have rescued civilians sitting in an empty bus than scattered around in an ongoing mass-casualty triage zone.

"You'll accompany the civilians behind me," I say pointing to the woman and children. "Walk with them, calmly and quietly, to the bus. And get back here as quickly as you can. We're about to receive a lot more people." They nod and set out.

I stay put, watching as the two soldiers accompany the family to the gas station. The look of terror in the little boy's eyes shook me. Gunfire, shouting in Arabic, and the sight of little children scarpering through the darkness past a mess of armored vehicles, searching for a safe place to escape to…. An abandoned bus at a ransacked gas station is all we have to offer them. Anger wells up inside me.

"Hi, can I borrow you for a second?" Suddenly, someone walks up to me—a lieutenant colonel, judging by his epaulets. "I see you're running the show. I'm a divisional medical officer."

"Hi. I'm Guy," I answer.

"I've just got one suggestion, and a minor comment," he says.

I frown, skeptical, tilting my head to one side. Who's this dude who's just shown up, hasn't even introduced himself, and is already handing out free advice?

"What's the comment?" I try to answer politely.

"Look," he says in a tone of stern disapproval, crossing his arms across his chest, "you can't evacuate casualties without taking their vital measurements, like pulse and blood pressure. You've got to perform a thorough triage before you start sending them to the helipad."

I feel fury raging up inside. Stress and fatigue are a pretty potent combination right now. My vocal cords get ready to unleash a roar, but my brain doesn't even know what argument to open with. How am I supposed to explain to him that he just doesn't understand how catastrophic the situation is? Maybe by pointing out I don't even have any medical equipment to treat the wounded? Or by telling him that if I perform triage and rank the casualties in terms of severity and urgency, I still have no way of treating them? Maybe I'll start with the fact we're under fire? Or the fact that we don't even have any vehicles to evacuate the wounded? Maybe I'll explain that it doesn't matter if the casualty's heartbeat is 50 or 200 because a mortar shell gets fired our way every few minutes, so I want to get all of them, whatever their condition, to a protected space as soon as possible?

I feel my pulse pounding in my temples. I don't even know what this guy's name is.

"Guy, more casualties!" shouts Smith.

In an instant, my attention switches. Like an over-inflated balloon, all the air rushes out of me in a heartbeat. I raise a thumb in the air, signaling to Smith that I heard him. Feldman runs over, stands to attention, and waits for instructions. The fact that he's back from the last helipad evacuation means that we now have an available ambulance.

I turn my gaze back to the medical officer, wondering again whether to rip into him. I choose to ignore his remark for now, and ask him to help us instead.

"We're evacuating the civilians who don't need medical attention to the gas station. Get someone to send buses to get them out," I say tersely and walk away.

I send the ambulances to the helipad, whatever random field that happens to be, and watch them speed away up the road. Soldiers with gunshot wounds from a shootout. One who'd had an arm blown off was crying with agony, a lump of flesh dangling from his shoulder. I try to get the horrific image out of my head by focusing on my breathing, concentrating my mind on what is yet to come.

The medical officer with the free advice comes back.

"The AMUs have arrived," he says proudly.

"AMUs? Great," I reply with a shrug, "but I've got no idea what that is." I'd guess that even the army's chief of staff discovers new acronyms every day.

"It stands for Aerial Medical Units. We've got excellent doctors. Surgeons and anesthesiologists. I think you should let them assess the casualties before evacuating them," he suggests, straightening his glasses on his nose. I nod, trying to stop my expression from giving away my skepticism about the idea.

"Look," I say, trying to soften my answer. "There are two options for the AMUs to get involved. First—"

Suddenly, a Red Alert rocket siren sounds. We throw ourselves on the ground, explosions reverberating all around us. I keep talking, still lying on the floor. "The AMUs can drive to the helipads and set up field hospitals there to treat the casualties while they're waiting for a 669 helicopter. Or they can join the medics in treating the casualties while they're evacuated to the helipads." I see from his facial expressions that the medical officer doesn't like the sound of either option.

Even while lying on our bellies, like lizards in the sand under mortar fire, I can already see where this conversation is going. In the background, we can hear the investigators shouting again, trying to extract some information from the prisoners.

The divisional medical officer comes right back at me. "What you suggest is impossible. The division commander won't approve splitting them up and won't authorize them to leave here."

I feel my patience running thin.

"Those are the two options. If you don't like them, then they can keep watching from the side." I then jump up, and stride away, I put on a façade of confidence, but I'm anything but sure. I'm full of doubt about whether I'm making a fatal mistake. Maybe I should actually hand over command to the officer on site, or to his supposed AMUs. After all, who am I? I spend my days sitting in the university medicine department and hearing lectures from real doctors. *Guy, trust your instincts*, I tell myself quietly.

Obviously I want assistance. I *need* assistance, considering the current crazy situation. But assistance needs to help the situation overall, not make it worse. If they want to set up a field hospital here, when we could come under fire from terrorists at any moment, with mortars landing randomly every few minutes, then that's on them. And if they want to screen the casualties, and measure their pulse and blood pressure, in the pitch dark, in the middle of a road, with tanks and APCs barreling along it in opposing directions, then I'd prefer to keep the situation as it is. If these AMUs aren't willing to get their hands dirty where it matters, then I'd rather stick with the volunteer Hatzalah guys. It's better for the casualties to be evacuated swiftly and efficiently to a helicopter than to have an AMU team making the mayhem all around us even more chaotic.

More casualties arrive. In the corner of my eye, I see the AMU soldiers and the medical officer standing to one side. They're watching us treat the casualties and load them into vehicles, dispatching them to the helipad. I hope deep down that the soldiers—in this case, reservists—will seize the reins. Within a short while, that's exactly what happens.

"Hi, I'm Nati," says one of the AMU guys, walking up to me. "We've heard the instructions of the division commander and the officer who's in charge of our unit. We've also had a chat between ourselves within the team. I'm the reservist commander, and we've got surgeons, anesthesiologists, and paramedics on site. We're all experienced. Forget the orders from above, we've come to work. Where do you need us?"

And so, in no time at all, I start assembling integrated teams of Hatzalah volunteer medics and AMU doctors. The teams wait by their vehicles, wearing military uniforms and fluorescent orange vests. A Satmar Hasidic Jew stands next to a secular Russian surgeon from the Sourasky Tel Aviv Medical Center, one explaining what he has in his ambulance, the other explaining where the medical equipment is in his military bag, and giving him pointers on trauma casualty care.

Finally, things on our end are starting to run smoother.

Two new casualties arrive.

We load them into the Hatzalah ambulances. Two AMU doctors, equipped with advanced trauma equipment, accompany each evacuation team. I can match free teams to incoming casualties. Out of the first armored vehicle comes a casualty with a crushed jaw. I load him onto the ambulance with an anesthesiologist. The second casualty took a bullet to his belly. I load him onto the ambulance with the general surgeon.

Feldman and Dan are sitting in the car up front, securing the convoy and getting them safely to the helipad. Shmuel is in charge of the Hatzalah volunteers while Nati runs the AMU teams. Smith is responsible for the access road, guiding tanks and pickup trucks transporting teams of soldiers in and out of the kibbutz, ensuring they won't block the main road along which casualties are flowing in and out.

I watch the scene like I'm observing it through a camera, and muster a limp smile. I feel the exhaustion spreading through my shoulders. The glands pumping out adrenaline all day are giving themselves a rest. I sit down on the ground praying that for a few minutes, there won't be any new casualties. I watch the scene from the side as traffic whizzes back and forth on the narrow access road to the kibbutz.

More teams of soldiers speed past me as reinforcements keep flooding into Kfar Aza. Military vehicles are full of young men who were only just conscripted next to grizzled reservists, some old enough to be the conscripts' fathers—or even grandfathers. Sitting in the driver's seat of the Hummer driving past me is a reservist sporting a white beard. From a glance, I'd guess he's at least fifty years old. Sitting in the back are young soldiers who, judging by their equipment, tactical vests, and weapons, seem not to have even finished their training yet. If not for the helmets on their heads, I'm sure I would be able to see a whole range of kippahs, bald heads, dreadlocks, and female soldiers' ponytails. I observe them. We make eye contact as they drive slowly past, joining the convoy heading inside as the vehicles leave dusty stripes across the asphalt.

In their eyes, I see grit laced with fear—the fear that any human being, maybe apart from a suicidal terrorist, must feel when danger lurks around every corner. That unique combination of determination and trepidation is alive in their eyes. As they drive slowly into the darkness that has settled on the terrorist-infested kibbutz, I don't even know if they realize that they're on their way to rescue civilians trapped in their homes.

Suddenly, I understand the big picture of what's happened: *Hamas must have attacked all the communities in the area.* I think about all my friends who live in nearby kibbutzim and towns. Sa'ad, Nir Oz, Meginim, Alumim, and more. I feel a wave of anxiety welling up inside me. I clamber to my feet. They might have all been murdered in their beds. I try to damp down the panic. *Guy, they're probably okay*, I tell myself. We heard on the news on the way here that a few hundred people were killed. *So, at least statistically speaking, they're probably okay.*

I take another look at the Hummer with the thickly-bearded driver, a second before he disappears into the darkness. His face is etched in my memory. I quietly pray that if I see him again tonight, it isn't wounded on a stretcher.

JUST A HI-TECH GUY

October 8th, 2023
00:30
Miller
Agricultural field on the side of the road,
The Gaza Envelope

So, there I am, urging the drivers of the ambulances and other improvised evacuation vehicles to head for places I've never heard of—Cheletz and Shuva—firmly emphasizing that that's where the helicopters are landing, and quietly praying to myself that these places really exist, and that the drivers won't be ambushed by terrorists on the way. While I'm directing the drivers, David Miller, my cohort's team leader (Cohort 42) and Oren Banda, my teammate, are working nonstop.

That morning, Miller had been woken up by the rocket sirens in his apartment in Ramat Gan, near Tel Aviv, which he'd only moved to recently following his wedding. He hurried down the staircase to the building's shared bomb shelter, and started reading the news on his phone. As he was swiping through news bulletins, Banda called.

"What the hell is happening?" Banda asks his commanding officer on reserves. Miller had been the commander of Cohort 42 when they went through training and had continued with the cohort from the pipeline into operational service and afterward to reserve duty.

"I'm only seeing the news now," Miller replies. "I'm thinking about heading to Tel Nof."

"Did they call us? What's it got to do with us?" asks Banda, who's part of the special ops team that Miller commands. The team gets called into reserve duty fairly frequently, and trains together more often than any other in the unit—but rocket attacks on the State of Israel isn't an incident that requires their unique set of skills.

"Well—no one's called," says Miller quietly. "But something doesn't feel right."

"So let's get going. Will you pick me up?" Banda interjects. As luck would have it, he'd just sold his car—he's due to go to Spain next week. His girlfriend is studying in Madrid, and he's planning to join her there and move to Europe.

A short while after they'd joined up with the unit, the two receive a mission and car keys. *Get there ASAP*—that's what they'd been told.

"Where is it?" Banda wonders aloud. "I've never heard of this place in my life."

"Me neither. Let's ask Waze," says Miller, and taps away at the app. And that's how, as night starts to fall, the two of them find themselves by the side of a road that runs between two towns in the Gaza Envelope, in the furrows of a plowed field that's been converted to a makeshift landing zone for the army's helicopters.

Over the past few hours, an unfathomable number of casualties have been brought in from all over the region. Pickup trucks with the injured laid across the cargo bed at the back; jeeps of all kinds; civilian ambulances. They all arrive with casualties of varying levels of severity.

Many of the vehicles bringing the injured here—or, to be more accurate, their drivers—have never encountered an army helicopter, and definitely not one that's landing in the dark, and that has no illumination equipment to flush out the terrorists nearby who are trying to take it down. A few hours ago, they heard a report of a helicopter that was shot down nearby. A terrorist fired a shoulder-launched missile at the helicopter while it was hovering just above the ground.

For now, Miller and Banda's role is to be in contact with the Unit 669 team members in the helicopter, informing them of the conditions of the waiting casualties, trying to ensure that the helicopter is on the ground for as little time as possible.

There's darkness all around them. They've just finished moving five casualties to the 669 helicopter when the mechanic closes the back hatch with a slam. The helicopter's blades stir up a dust storm in the gloom of the night, throwing specks of earth into the air in all directions, and almost uprooting the thick bushes that surround the plowed field. Banda shields his head with his right forearm, defending himself from the mud flying through the air, as the helicopter takes flight and is swallowed up by the night.

With the helicopter safely airborne, he and Miller walk briskly back to the edge of the field, toward their parked car.

"We have to make sure that the blankets covering the casualties are zipped onto the stretcher poles. The one that was covering the first casualty almost flew into the engine," Miller says, conducting a quick debrief to make sure they improve for the next time round. Banda pulls a water bottle out of the trunk of the car, takes a few gulps, and passes it to Miller. He's shaking out his shirt vigorously, trying to get rid of the specks of dirt that made it past his neck and are now stuck to his sweat-ridden back.

"Do we have a spare battery for the comms device?" he asks, suddenly remembering that the one currently in use is on its last legs.

Miller rummages around in the trunk of the army car. "Yeah, there are two more full batteries," he announces triumphantly. Their ability to carry out any more missions is dependent on the battery supply; that's what will let them stay in contact with the unit, Air Force central command and—most importantly—with the helicopters.

The radio crackles to life. "Did someone call for Wildcats?" broadcasts Miller in response. No answer. Given that there are so many casualties in different parts of the region, as soon as the helicopter team has managed to transfer their injured to a hospital, they're straight back in the air, returning to the Gaza Envelope. That means that the Air Force Command is sending a helicopter on its next mission mid-flight, without it ever coming back to base. It's like Uber Eats during peak hours. The only possible reason that a helicopter wouldn't be either on the way to collect casualties or to a hospital would be if it had run out of fuel.

"Look." Miller directs Banda's attention to the flashing lights approaching them from the road.

"This is Wildcats, I have casualties on the ground at the landing area. Is there a helicopter on the way?" asks Miller over the radio.

At the same time, Banda uses his phone to call up Command, trying to find out how long it'll be until the next helicopter arrives. He knows every minute counts. The operatives at central command that are directing operations must be under a huge amount of pressure—but they have to give their attention over to making sure there's a helicopter on the way.

No one answers the phone.

From the road, three Hatzalah ambulances and an army jeep pull in. Banda flashes his light, indicating for them to slow down.

The convoy comes to a stop.

Banda and Miller rush over to the vehicles, and a familiar figure gets out of one of them. Banda recognizes Feldman—he led his marine rescue training, as he does every year with the teams in the pipeline. As you might have expected from a religious guy like Feldman, he was never the group's strongest swimmer, but he always exemplified staying composed and coolheaded.

"What did you bring us?" Banda shouts to him, momentarily dazzled by the vehicles' bright headlights searing through the dark.

"Three seriously injured, two lightly," he replies.

"Miller, got that?" asks Banda, to ensure that Miller relays the info to the helicopter. For five casualties, two helicopters would be ideal. But tonight, nothing is anywhere close to ideal.

"Feldman, let's go talk to the Hatzalah medics—I want to make sure they know how to rush to the chopper as soon as it lands."

As Banda finishes speaking, central command confirms that a helicopter is on its way. Miller tries to make contact with the crew on board.

"*Wildcats, this is Eagles, do you copy?*" The voice of a helicopter pilot sounds through the radio.

"Roger that," replies Miller. "How long till you're with me?"

"*Five minutes tops.*"

Banda, meanwhile, is circulating among the ambulances, and realizes that unlike previous occasions, in every ambulance there's a reservist next to each Hatzalah member: doctors, paramedics—and advanced medical equipment.

"Who are they?" he asks Feldman.

"They're from the AMU," Feldman answers, using an acronym Banda doesn't recognize.

"AMU?"

"Beats me, they might be the…Alternative Medicine Unit?" says Feldman with a smile.

"So many acronyms…" mutters Banda, heading into one of the ambulances. "There's a helicopter landing in four minutes, be ready to transfer the casualty," he says to the Hatzalah medic who's sitting beside the AMU doctor.

Inside the army jeep are three kids, coughing loudly. A Hatzalah medic is giving one of them oxygen. Banda hands them all earplugs. "We're about to transfer you all to the helicopter. It'll be pretty loud."

The engine roar that approaches from the east heralds the arrival of the helicopter. The aircraft moves invisibly through the darkness and touches down in a matter of a few moments, and the rescue team members burst out into the night through its back door.

"Banda! What's up?" shouts Winnick, emerging from the darkness. He too had been trained by Banda on the marine rescue course.

"You won't believe the day we've had," Banda answers, his mind scrambled. "I feel like we're in a novel, like a character in some thriller that you pick up at the airport. I'm wiped already from all the action."

As the rescue soldiers bring the casualties out of the ambulances, the helicopter's medical personnel exchange a few sentences with the members of the AMU medical team to get a sense of their condition and what treatment they've already had.

"Stomach wound, start by giving him blood," says Hannah to Winnick at the doorway of the second ambulance. He gets to work, and he and the ambulance crew move the casualty out of the vehicle and hurry him over to the helicopter.

Within three minutes, all of the casualties are safely loaded into the belly of the helicopter. "Looks like we'll see you again soon," says Barnea, breaking into a light jog and joining the rest of his team, who are already working intensively to treat the casualties.

Banda replies by way of a light salute.

A few seconds later, there's a shout from behind them.

"Wait a sec!" yells Feldman, cupping his radio to his ear. "There's another casualty on the way."

"How long till he gets here?" asks Miller. "There are always casualties on the way. That's a given."

"Just a few minutes. He's in deep shock, he lost a lot of blood."

Miller takes a deep breath. He must make a quick decision: keep the helicopter on the ground or let it go.

"Eagle from Wildcats," he says over the radio, hoping he's not delaying the helicopter for nothing. Aside from the danger it's in here on the ground, there are casualties that need to get to the hospital straight away.

No answer.

"Eagle, Eagle, do you copy?"

The mechanic's already closing the ramp at the back.

"The casualty is a few hundred feet away," Feldman updates Miller over the radio. *"He's got a massive hemorrhage; they can't stop it."*

"Eagle, Eagle, come in," Miller radios, trying again to call the helicopter's crew. *Damn comms systems.* He sees flashing lights approaching from the direction of the road. The casualty really is here—but the helicopter blades are already accelerating. It will be airborne within seconds. And a helicopter that's taken off isn't coming back.

"For God's sake," snaps Banda, and breaks into a sprint. His long legs scythe along the ground like sharp scissors, snapping through the field over the long furrows of earth.

"What are you doing??" Miller shouts at him, grimacing as globules of earth, whipped into a frenzy by the accelerating helicopter blades, come flying toward him through the air. Banda keeps up his sprint toward the ramp, and Miller wonders if he's planning to grab onto the helicopter himself and, hanging in mid-air, somehow prevent it from taking off.

"Hey! Stop!!" screams Banda, knowing that the chance of actually being heard is close to zero. He needs someone in the helicopter to see him, for the mechanic or one of the combat soldiers to recognize his figure and get the pilot to stop.

Banda sees the silhouette of a figure at the helicopter entrance, under the rear blades, signalling with rapid hand gestures: *get back!*

He doesn't stop. Arriving at the ramp, he yells in the direction of the mechanic.

"There's another casualty!"

Apparently, the mechanic didn't hear what Banda had said. Barnea emerges from the interior of the helicopter and jumps down from the ramp.

"What's the problem?" he shouts, confused.

"There's another casualty!" Banda screams into his ear.

Miller, meanwhile, who'd seen that Banda had managed to stop the helicopter taking off, had already gotten the casualty out of the ambulance, working with the army doctors and Hatzalah medics, and all of them are already rushing toward the helicopter. The casualty looks to be in bad shape. Blood is dripping from the stretcher. He seems to have a serious facial wound, and has lost consciousness.

The mechanic finishes lowering the ramp at exactly the moment that the stretcher arrives. The team is already occupied treating the other casualties, so Miller and the other medics carrying the stretcher head into the helicopter. They set it down on the chopper floor, amongst the other stretchers, and run out again.

Miller is left standing in the middle of the field, breathing heavily from the exertion, his hands resting on his thighs. Sweat is pouring down his face.

"I think in the last hour, I've seen more casualties than during my entire service in the unit," he says to Banda, who's slowly coming toward him.

"Yeah, no doubt. Same," Banda murmurs back.

There's a thought running through Banda's head. He decides to share it with Miller.

"This whole night feels like a drill in our training course. Like we're back in time."

"You bastard, you're not even out of breath!" gasps Miller, ignoring Banda's reflection on the moment and feeling more irritated that he is in such good shape.

Banda ignores him. "It's really like it was in training," he continues. "With every casualty, there's another dilemma; there's a catch, some sort of complication that forces you to make a quick decision."

Now, Miller's pleased. "Looks like your commanders on your training course knew what they were doing. Remind me who your team leader was?" he asks, playing dumb.

"Meh, some guy—can't remember his name anymore," responds Banda, wrapping his long arm around Miller's shoulders. "He used to be this player who would hit on any girl in Tel Aviv with a heartbeat. These days, he's some hi-tech guy that lives in the suburbs, growing a beer belly."

I SHOULD HAVE DONE IT MYSELF

October 8th, 2023
01:00
Guy
Kfar Aza

A car speeds up the access road toward the kibbutz, and Smith waves his arms up and down in the middle of the road, signaling for it to slow down and pull over to the side. Even at this point in the night, vehicles are racing toward our triage station at dangerous speeds. It's like a rescue mission siren going off at 669 headquarters, except here, and the speeding cars are not the note to run to the helicopter, but rather the harbinger of casualties coming to you. The doors open and the driver helps a few children out. "We got them out of a burned building," he says. "There was smoke everywhere."

I ask them how they are. One of them is hoarse. The other has a cough. I'm worried about burns in their airways and smoke inhalation injuries. I shine my flashlight into the mouth of the kid with the cough. He looks to be around eight years old, maybe ten.

"The terrorists are using gas cylinders to set the houses on fire," says a voice behind me. "They're cutting the gas pipes and lighting them up."

The children look mainly exhausted rather than seriously harmed. The coughing continues. Meanwhile, Shmuel from Hatzalah walks over to me.

"Guy, a mobile intensive care unit will be here any minute as backup for the ambulances with our medics." I nod, thinking to myself, *it couldn't have been here ten hours earlier?* But before I can finish checking the children, another car pulls up next to me. A man steps out of the passenger seat, holding two babies. Infants wrapped in blankets. I reach out to take them from him. Immediately, I think better of it. I'm wearing black gloves, or, in army lingo, tactical gloves: cloth gloves that leave my fingertips exposed. My hands are completely red. There is such a thick layer of blood on my hands that even the black gloves look red. The material is still wet, and it's not from water. I call one of the female Hatzalah volunteers and ask her to take the babies.

"What happened to them?" I ask the man, as I quickly check them over. They seem fine, all in all.

"We found them hidden in a closet," he answers. I want to go back and double-check the children again, wondering whether—and how—to evacuate them right now when suddenly, another Red Alert siren screams through the night. A barrage of interceptor rockets lights up the night sky like fireworks, and we hit the ground, Feldman and Dan covering the children with their bodies. Powerful explosions, followed by exchanges of fire ringing out from nearby buildings in the kibbutz. A horrific sound that we're already used to. It might as well be elevator music.

Another car races toward us, this time a hulking armored military vehicle. The doors open, and two seriously injured soldiers roll out. One is missing an arm and the other has a gruesome facial injury.

"Get the kids out of here!" I shout at some of the soldiers standing nearby. "The soldier with the facial wounds—to the first ambulance. The other casualty—try to put a tourniquet above the amputation and get him in the second ambulance."

I direct the soldiers around me. "Nati, get the guys in the cars," I bark at the commander from the AMUs.

"We've got another one!" shouts a voice from the darkened back seat of the massive vehicle. I clamber in. Lying between the seats is a middle-aged man. Bleeding from his hip, he's extremely pale but still conscious.

"Put this casualty in the ambulance with the amputee, lie him down on the bench." The combined AMU-Hatzalah team pops up behind me, and together we set the injured man down on a stretcher. "Okay, get to the helipad!" I urge the ambulance drivers.

Suddenly, Avinoam, the division's medical officer—the one with the free advice and bad attitude—walks up to me, holding a radio. "Guy, in a moment, you're going receive a truck full of casualties and the bodies of soldiers from a nearby base," he says quietly.

"Okay," I say distractedly, acknowledging the update with a slight nod, as if he's just told me it might rain tomorrow and I shouldn't plan to hit the beach. It feels as though nothing can surprise me anymore. At least, that's what I'd thought.

"Cohen, Smith, come here!" I call both of them over. They stand in front of me. "There's a truck that's supposed to get here soon, with bodies and casualties. When it arrives, take it to the edge of that row of trees, where the bodies are. Just make sure the civilians here don't see what's coming out." I point to the people by the roadside who are making their way to the gas station, escorted by Elazar's men.

Smith and Cohen nod. I look at them, thinking about what I just said—that we need to protect the civilians from witnessing these horrors. But what about Smith and Cohen themselves? They were civilians until just a few hours ago too, right up until they threw on their uniforms and showed up for reserves—don't they need protecting?

Don't I?

"Guy, there's another car coming!" Dan shouts to me. Smith directs it toward us so that it won't crash into the incoming tank from across the intersection.

"The truck we spoke about?" I ask, confused.

"Not a truck, dude. A car! Casualties!"

I look behind me. An APC is speeding my way. I look in the other direction. The ambulances have just departed for the helipad—and, in any case, they have no room for more casualties. The doors of the APC open. In the doorway is a soldier holding a girl, seven years old at most. She's clearly suffering from breathing difficulties. "What's wrong with her?" I ask.

"Severe asthma attack."

I am not sure I heard him right. We're at war. Casualties. Gunfire. Where the hell did this little girl with asthma come from?

I shove my hands under her armpits, carry her in my arms, and sit her on the chilly curbside. She must be cold, I think to myself, and smile at her, trying to put on a calm face. During an asthma attack, stress only makes things worse. God only knows where they found this girl and what she saw. She looks bad. Her eyelids are already half-closed. She needs oxygen and medication. She needs a mobile intensive care unit. She might even need ventilation right now.

I feel despair coursing through me, but I use every muscle in my body to hold that smile on my face, looking into her eyes, which are glazing over. Her airways have narrowed; carbon dioxide is building up in her blood, causing her to start losing consciousness. I keep smiling with everything I've got, but inside, I'm crying. This little girl is suffocating in front of my eyes. I cradle her, and she leans on me, her warm breath steaming on my shoulder.

Then, I hear another car approaching. I look at the junction with the main road. The Hatzalah mobile intensive care unit is heading our way. "Just in time!" I say out loud. A doctor steps out of the vehicle. I call out to her.

"Do you have Ventolin? Steroids? Adrenaline? Basically, anything for asthma?" I ask the doctor. She nods and I hand her the girl. I walk away, my smile still stretched across my face.

I look for Cohen. I want to ask him to ride with the mobile intensive care unit to secure it, but I can't find him in the darkness. I ask the people around me whether anyone has seen the guys from Unit 669.

"I saw them walking with one of the ambulance people there," says one soldier, pointing at the row of trees. "They were leading a truck of some sort." I gulp. *There must be a body, maybe two*, I tell himself. *They'll be back in a moment, and you'll find the right dark joke. Something to lighten the atmosphere.*

Before going over to examine what's in the truck, I take advantage of the temporary breather, and reiterate to anyone around me with epaulets or comms gear that there are civilians at the gas station who are waiting to be evacuated. I emphasize that they're desperately waiting for some mode of transportation to whisk them away to safety.

Suddenly, I see Cohen and Smith, both of them slowly walking back up the road toward the main triage area. I run over to them. They stop. I wait for one of them to say something first. Unbearable silence. I place my hand gently on Cohen's shoulder, putting an arm around him in a gentle clasp, and giving him a slight shake.

"You okay?" I ask quietly. I lock eyes with Smith, then back to Cohen. Their faces are pale. Sweat is dripping down Cohen's shirt.

"It was horrible," Smith says. I wait a couple of seconds. An uncomfortable silence begins to set in, but I give them the time they need. "There were people I know. There were two guys…corpses…that were a few years younger than me in school." He drops his gaze.

"So many bodies…" adds Cohen. "So many body parts…"

I take a deep breath. The pain on Cohen's face is palpable. He purses his lips, as if trying to hold back those horrific scenes, the trauma he's just endured in unloading that truck full of gruesome death, as if his mouth is a dam about to burst. His hands are shaking slightly.

"I'm so sorry you had to go through that," I say. But this time, I can't stop my own tears. They well up in my eyes, and suddenly, it's my dam that's burst. Salty teardrops run down my filthy cheeks and nose. My face was already drenched in sweat, and flecked with dirt and blood.

"It's okay, it's part of our mission," says Cohen tersely. His lips curl into a smile, but it's completely hollow. There isn't a single spark of joy in his expression. I look away. Now my face is tensed up too, as I try to halt the tears — even though I don't really know why I should stop them.

I wipe my eyes and step away from Cohen and Smith, angry at myself. I was so focused on trying to protect the residents leaving the kibbutz, to spare them the horrors arriving by the carload every few minutes and to keep them safe. But what's the difference between the refugees huddled at the gas station, on the one hand, and Cohen and Smith on the other? Those two are civilians too, aren't they? They're definitely not on their mandatory service anymore. They're regular guys whose lives are full of regular worries. Girlfriends, work, rent, plans for the future. They threw on their uniforms a few hours ago and raced south. Does that make them soldiers now? Does that mean that they now have to pay the price instead of someone else? For the rest of their lives, they'll be haunted by the horrendous things they've seen today. Sleepless nights filled with nightmares; rushes of adrenaline whenever a motorbike backfires, reminding them of the explosions going off in the background every few minutes.

I can't shake their ashen, zombie-like expressions. Smith's almost slurred speech. Cohen's vacant expression. I told them to do this. I ordered them to unload a truck full of their dead friends' bodies in the dark, alone. *What on earth was I thinking?* I should have been there. I should have unloaded the truck myself.

My train of thought gets cut off in an instant as reality jerks me back to the present.

"Guys, come on over, we've brought reinforcements," shouts one of the Hatzalah volunteers. He opens the door of the ambulance, revealing a pile of pizza boxes. Cardboard boxes from some local pizzeria, just like the ones we used to order at high school in Tiberias for seven dollars a box, proudly bearing the slogan: THE CHEAPEST IN TOWN!

I feel like my stomach is giving a ten-gun salute. I haven't eaten anything since last night, though I have been fantasizing about the sandwiches Noga's mom threw me this morning. I can't believe I left them in the car.

"Wow, wow, what a treat!" Cohen says, with genuine gratitude.

"Thank you very much," I add, giving the man handing out the pizza a hearty thump on the shoulder, though I want to crush him in a bear hug. The smell of melted cheese fills my nostrils like perfume.

"My absolute pleasure. Eat up boys," he says.

I prop my pizza box on the sidewalk and sit next to it. I grab a slice and fold it to stop the olives from sliding off. A long cord of cheese stretches from the slice all the way back to the box on the curb. I glance to the side and smile at the sight of Cohen and Smith going to town on their pizza. Refocusing, I bring the slice up to my mouth, but stop before the first bite. A sharp metallic odor fills my nostrils, wafting off my bloodstained hands. It's my cloth gloves. My fingertips, pinching the fluffy dough, are still glistening red, with congealed bloodstains covering my hands like varnish. I hesitate for a moment.

Who are you kidding? I think to myself. *Today's not the day.* I take a bite of the pizza, relishing it more than anything else I've ever eaten. I chew slowly. This must be the best pizza I've ever had. *It's even enriched with iron.* I grin to myself, strangely satisfied by my own dark sense of humor.

I spot Feldman heading back from the helipad.

"Come eat some pizza!" I call to him, inviting him over to our new curbside cafeteria. He sits down next to me.

"What's up? Heard anything from the unit?" I ask him, reaching out to grab another slice.

"From what I gathered in the last phone call," he says, carefully selecting a slice of pizza, "when we wrap up here—whenever that is—we need to get to Kibbutz Be'eri."

THE NIGHT WILL PROTECT YOU

October 8th, 2023
03:00
Guy
The entrance to Kibbutz Be'eri

We turn at the junction, a few minutes after the sign tells us to take a right to Kibbutz Be'eri. It's pitch black, but the road leading to the kibbutz is full of cars.

"Go as far as you can," I tell Dan. "You can overtake the Hummer from the right." I point to a Hummer parked by the roadside, so wide that it almost blocks the entire road. He drives cautiously and finally parks our pickup truck on the sidewalk next to the access road.

We get out of the car, and the staccato sound of gunfire erupting from somewhere nearby welcomes us onto the scene. Judging by the sound, it's only a few hundred feet away at most. We walk along the row of trees, toward what looks like a sandy parking lot next to the gates of the kibbutz. I try to remember if I've ever visited Be'eri. I don't think so, but it's possible I came here once and don't remember. It's the middle of the night and I'm not thinking clearly; I've been running on fumes for a while.

"Look at all the bodies…." whispers Dan, gesturing at the hedgerow encircling the parking lot. Long shadows are arranged all across the area, lying there in the darkness, sprawled in contorted positions, wearing tatters of clothes and shoes. I nod apathetically and keep walking, like they're candy wrappers left behind by hikers on a nature trail.

"What's going on here?" I ask quietly, without waiting for an answer. I hear a commotion, not far from us. After what we've already seen, I didn't think anything could surprise us. So much for that idea.

Near the kibbutz gates, next to the low fence by the parking lot, are dozens of civilians. I assume they're local residents. There's a woman perched on a small rock, and in the gloomy torchlight, she looks old—maybe eighty, even, like my grandma. She's sitting in the darkness, her arms crossed, as if hugging her own body, with her back straight but her head dropping. It looks like she's sleeping. But when I pace past her, I hear her sobbing. I hesitate, slow down, and stop for a moment, wondering whether I should approach her. Her muffled cries are heartbreaking. I feel a lump rising in my throat, just from hearing her sob. I stand there, torn over whether to walk up to the old lady or not, but then, luckily, another woman approaches her anyway. She wraps her arms around the grandmother's shoulders and I allow myself to move on. I look around. It looks like everyone's waiting for something, waiting to be told where to go.

These civilians must have all been evacuated because there are still terrorists in the kibbutz. We advance toward what looks like the heart of the action. Naively, I assume we're talking about a handful of terrorists—at this point, we still have no idea as to the magnitude of the ongoing incident. I couldn't have imagined that over one hundred terrorists had been running amok in the kibbutz, slaughtering the local residents and going neighborhood to neighborhood and house to house in search of victims.

I'll discover the unimaginable truth about what happened here soon enough.

In the parking lot, I meet Carmel, a Unit 699 officer in mandatory service. "What's up?" he says, extending a tired hand.

"We're here to help," I reply, extending my own, still wearing that filthy glove. The guys look shattered. Parked in this narrow sandy patch, between the trees—cypresses or pines, it's impossible to tell in the darkness—is a row of ambulances, mostly military. *Why did these teams not come to Kfar Aza?* I wonder to myself.

"There's still active combat in various sections of the kibbutz," Carmel briefs me. "We keep getting fresh casualties."

"Who's in charge of processing the casualties?" I ask him.

He points to four people, three men and a woman, standing next to a row of unfurled stretchers. Two of them have stethoscopes around their necks. There's a sea of wrappers from medical equipment scattered on the ground, a synthetic lawn of translucent plastic.

"Who's the one in charge? Who's responsible for the order of evacuation? You can't have four people commanding—" I begin to insist. But before I can close my mouth, an APC speeds into view. It stops with a screech in the sandy parking lot. The doors open. I know the drill. I stop myself from getting involved. I've just arrived; I'm the newbie, and it looks like they have enough medical forces already on the scene. I don't want to get in the way.

Three wounded soldiers. Gunshot wounds. One to his chest, the others to their limbs. "Get that injured soldier over here!" someone shouts.

"No, no, lie them down somewhere else," someone else shouts.

"Why not straight to the ambulance?" a third person suggests.

Meanwhile, in all the chaos, the casualties make their way somehow to the open stretchers. The medical staff starts treating them. It's clear that everyone is exhausted.

I spot one of the casualties lying alone, without anyone by his side. I kneel next to his stretcher. "What's up?" I ask him.

"The motherfuckers shot me," the soldier says, hoarse. He has gunshot wounds all along his right arm, with a tourniquet above his elbow. I help him remove his tactical vest.

"Did they hit you anywhere else?" I ask him. He's conscious, lucid—and he looks extremely familiar. I can see that he's tall and broad-shouldered, even though he's supine on a stretcher.

"No, just my arm. I've checked myself," he says in a tone that snipes: *don't touch me.* I offer him some painkillers. He refuses. And then he screams.

It's not a cry of pain, but of anger. Of frustration. Suddenly, I realize where I know him from. The pointy gray beard that extracted casualties in Kfar Aza! I look over his injuries quickly, to check that the bleeding has stopped.

"Who can help me carry this stretcher?" I call out. There's no point keeping him waiting on the ground. There are enough parked ambulances.

"No stretcher! I don't need anyone to carry me. I can walk by myself," he announces and tries to pick himself up on his feet.

"No, no," I snap, stopping him and pushing him back down. Who knows where else he might have been hit? His whole body is covered in shrapnel. He might have taken more rounds in other places. I don't want to take the risk that this fearless warrior's adrenaline is concealing a more serious injury.

"I need you on the stretcher. It'll be easier that way for us to get you in an ambulance," I tell him. "It's not for you, dude, it's for us." I hope I've convinced him; at least *I'm* satisfied with my own improvised argument. I can see him wrestling with himself, but eventually he gives up and lies back down.

We load him into an ambulance and I close the doors. "Off you go!" I shout to the driver up front.

"Where's Guy?" I hear Feldman's voice cutting through the darkness. "We need to move. We've been given a mission."

"We've got to enter the kibbutz and find people trapped in their homes."

CAUTION: KIBBUTZNIK AHEAD

October 8th, 2023
04:30
Ron and Tamar
The young people's neighborhood on Meginim

While Feldman and I get into our Toyota, a few miles away on Kibbutz Meginim, the all-clear signal is finally given. The people there can now start leaving their homes.

All of the terrorists have been eliminated, and now the residents are being evacuated. It's like the Exodus. People are flocking out of their homes, carrying precious few possessions, on the move without knowing where they're headed or when they'll return. Ron's father has linked up with the commander of the company that encircled the kibbutz. Ron goes back to his apartment.

So many of the cars on the kibbutz have been damaged in combat with the terrorists that the surviving residents are being evacuated on board buses instead. They were asked to take only a few, truly essential belongings. They had to hunker down in their houses for nearly twenty hours during the onslaught; only in the afternoon did robust army forces start to arrive on the scene. Armed fighters from various units, including the police and even the prison services, reached the kibbutz and eliminated terrorists, who were making their last stand in by-then fortified positions. Ron and Tamar, together with a combat engineering team, went house to house, family to family, to ensure that no more terrorists were hiding in the kibbutz.

The kibbutz had only been declared under our forces' control once an entire company of reinforcements had been deployed along the length of the perimeter fence, around dusk, taking up defensive positions against another possible enemy infiltration. Only then were the residents instructed to leave their homes.

Ron and Tamar have been helping the kibbutz evacuate. Their neighbors and friends, tears in their eyes, are all frantically packing suitcases in a daze, before being crammed into cars and driven away. Although they have been told that it's safe to leave the kibbutz, nobody believes it. Only a few hours ago, they saw terrorists crossing their own backyards—so who can guarantee them that there are no more in the area, lying in wait among the trees and playgrounds? It doesn't help that they're being told to hurry up and pack, with no clue when they can return, and that they're being taken off to some hotel in some other part of the country, with no indication of when they'll be able to return.

This is a kibbutz whose members were immensely proud that in multiple previous rounds of fighting with the Gaza terror organizations, even when the tanks and artillery cannons roared overhead, their tractors always reached the fields to reap the harvest at the right time. Even when mortars came crashing down like the first rains of winter, there were always people working in the kibbutz's factory. *You never abandon your home, even when you have to fight for it*, they vowed to themselves. And now, for the first time, even the most fierce-spirited and gritty kibbutzniks who built the community, even the war heroes, even the Holocaust survivors who escaped to here from Europe, all of them, without exception, have been forced to leave their homes. Besides Ron's father and a few other members of the civilian defense forces, who've stayed behind to help the company of paratroopers, everyone has been evacuated to a hotel.

A massive explosion erupts in the distance.

"What was that?" asks Ron.

"Must be an airstrike," Tamar assumes. She has no idea that ferocious battles are still raging in Be'eri and Kfar Aza, just a few miles away.

The pair walk slowly down the narrow path from the road to their neighborhood. The citrus trees exude a pungent smell. Sounds of explosions and gunfire reverberate through the air. Their gaits slow with tiredness as they quietly make their way back to their rooms. Red streaks across the sky from the east, signaling the onset of dawn, which quickly claims yesterday's lost territory from the receding darkness of the night. Although it's barely been twenty-four hours since Ron woke Tamar up, he feels like it's been years since he last slept. The weapons slung around his shoulders, his M16 and the co-opted Kalashnikov, clang together to the tempo of their steps.

"Hey, what happened to Chaim in the end? Did he reach a hospital?" asks Tamar, interrupting the silence.

"Yup. I heard someone say that two guys from 669 were in an open field nearby. They got helicopters to land there one by one, like it was an airport. They evacuated him and John, too. None of the other Thai workers survived."

A pause sets in. Then Ron carries on.

"I heard there were attacks on other communities too. Wonder when the army reached them." *Fifteen minutes and the army will arrive to take control of the situation*, he can still hear reverberating in his mind. *You just need to hold your ground for fifteen minutes*.

"Hopefully it was the same as us: they arrived late but the civilian defense forces were able to hold them off at least," says Tamar.

"Yeah, I guess that's what happened," Ron agrees, his voice weak. He stops at the entrance to his apartment. In front of the rickety wooden door, covered in countless stickers with kibbutz movement slogans. The layers have piled up over the years. AGRICULTURE WILL PREVAIL. DRINK ISRAELI MILK. CAUTION: KIBBUTZNIK AHEAD. COME VISIT: SOUTH IN BLOOM.

Faint black lines across the concrete, skid marks, remind him that he needs to pick up his moped, still behind the minimarket.

"Your mom might donate that moped to the army, it's her chance to get rid of it," quips Tamar, practically reading his mind. They both stand glued to the spot, looking around. Tamar pulls her hair into a scrunchie.

Ron finds a packet of cigarettes on the table in the communal chillout area. He lights a cigarette and inhales deeply into his lungs. Tamar gestures to him to pass it, and puffs deeply on the lit cigarette.

"You realize there were literally terrorists here, in the kibbutz?" Tamar mumbles, puffing out a thick haze into the chilly morning air.

"Nope, it hasn't registered. Still doesn't feel real," Ron answers, feeling desperate for a shower. He stinks of smoke and sweat and fear and pigeon poop. His muscles hurt from a combination of exhaustion and being in pure survival mode. It's a sensation he knows well from the army, but it feels so strange in this environment, in the tranquil and safe surroundings of the kibbutz. He feels a whirlwind of emotions, his tiredness only making everything spin more wildly. It's like his body has been denying all the fear and pain, and now, suddenly, it's all been let loose.

He's desperate to speak to his mother. To tell her what happened, how freaked out he'd been, how scared he'd been. And to tell her that he was also proud of himself. The only thing he'd like to do right now more than crawl into bed and pass out would be to sit next to her at the kitchen table. She'd make him a cup of tea with some mint from the beige potted plant outside the front door. She'd pull the cookie jar out from the pantry, open it, and place it in the center of their table. That was their routine.

But that definitely wasn't going to happen today. She'd accompanied all the neighbors, figuring out who was traveling in a car and who by bus, making sure that everyone in the community had somewhere to sleep tonight at that hotel they were heading toward, that someone had managed to arrange.

"Right, I'm off to sleep," he says, stubbing out his half-finished cigarette, as if forcing himself to wrap up and go back to his room.

"We should catch some sleep. A couple of hours," she says, nodding, her eyes red. Her uniform is tattered. She shifts weight from side to side anxiously.

But then they both stay put, completely silent.

Finally, Tamar turns around and heads back to her room.

"Good night," Ron mumbles and heads into his darkened apartment.

It's almost sunrise, but the blinds are still closed from the night before, and his bed is still messy from his frantic wake-up. Ron takes off the uniform he borrowed from Tamar and chucks it on the floor near the bathroom. He rests his gun under his pillow—an old habit from sleeping out in the field during his military service. He wonders whether to take a shower. He really wants to, but tiredness gets the better of him and he makes do with washing his face.

Ron's eyes are half-closed but his body is primed, his muscles tensed up. He gets into bed and under the blanket, resting his head on the pillow. He takes a deep breath and shuts his eyes. Then, as though the play button was pressed for a movie, scenes from the past day flash in front of his eyes. Terrorists at the fence. Yair being shot and crumpling on the living room table. The Thai workers, riddled with bullets. He opens his eyes in a panic, his heart racing. *Ron, you need to calm down*, he tells himself. *Everything's okay. The army's here. You're in your bedroom, in your own bed.* He tries again, taking a deep breath and closing his eyes.

Suddenly, he hears the door hinges screech and jolts up, reaching out to grab his gun tucked under his head. Tamar appears in the doorway, wearing a polo shirt and shorts. Without saying a word, she lies down on the bed next to Ron and pulls the edge of the blanket over her body. Tamar shuts her eyes and turns her head, and Ron slides the pillow out underneath her head. Tamar's breaths caress his neck. They rub shoulders. Her body heat calms him down. He feels his muscles relaxing and his feverish thoughts starting to subside.

"When we get up, let's go help your dad with the cows?" she asks him suddenly, as if mumbling in her sleep. "Someone's got to help him milk them."

"Sure, that's a good idea," he replies, closing his eyes and sinking into a deep sleep.

THE GUYS WHO REALLY WIN WARS

October 8th, 2023
05:00
Guy
The center of Be'eri

Through our pickup truck's windows, the carnage is clear. Smoke billows from the rubble of people's houses. The headlights illuminate cars burned to ashes. Straight ahead of us, a tank emerges out of the darkness like a monster from a nightmare. It crosses the road and turns down a narrow path running through the lawn in front of a row of homes, engulfing a sidewalk designed for bicycles and mobility scooters. I stare at the war machine in astonishment. Its massive treads crush everything in their path and spit out debris like crumpled paper. Bushes, bicycle racks, street signs. The tank's turret jerks from side to side like an elephant's trunk while it slowly moves between the houses.

"Can you see anything?" asks Feldman, who's sitting up front next to Dan. Another person joined us too, I think his name is Rafi. I've already given up on trying to remember names. Every few hours, I found myself in a different place, on a different mission with different people, different units. Calling everyone "bro" is good enough. "Keep your eyes open. Say something if you detect any signs of life. It should be around here," says Rafi. "This is where we got the intel about civilians trapped in their homes."

Our aging vehicle sputters. We just got back from dropping off a couple at the entrance of the kibbutz, local residents that had been hiding at home and couldn't leave until now. Initially, we were told that there were wounded soldiers in the area—a squad got ambushed and couldn't get out of the kibbutz by themselves. But during the search for the casualties, we found this couple, who were literally trapped in their apartment. I looked them over quickly; they didn't seem to have any injuries—at least not on the outside. Psychologically? Well, that's something else entirely.

Continuing our search for additional casualties, we drive past a row of single-level houses. I give the scene a visual sweep through the windows, scouring for any movement in the darkness. Suddenly, the sharp drumming of gunfire impacts the back part of the Toyota . I jump out of my seat, tensing up in panic in the back of the vehicle.

"Don't stop!" barks Feldman at Dan. "We're here to rescue casualties, not get into a gunfight with the enemy! The tanks can take care of the terrorists, believe me, they're the guys who really win wars…. Hang on, slow down, it should be here somewhere."

He's holding his cell phone, his face lit up from the glow of Google Maps. I realize we're navigating to a pin sent via WhatsApp to his personal device.

Dan stops in the middle of the narrow path. There's no point trying to park; the path and turf all around us has been ripped to shreds by tanks, all sorts of armored vehicles, and a day of intense combat.

"Guy, this time, hold back and secure the vehicle," says Feldman, as he and Dan clamber out and over to the nearest building. I stay back outside the car. I'm down on one knee, sweeping the scene, feeling totally exposed and vulnerable. Apart from me in the middle of the road, the area is deserted, all the buildings abandoned and rid-dled with bullet holes. Walls collapsing in on themselves. Whole rooms reduced to charred pillars of concrete.

The first ray of dawn melts the darkness, slowly revealing the magnitude of the carnage. Every building around me is a pile of rubble. I realize that the rapidly spreading daylight makes me a more prominent target. Every movement could be a Hamas sniper about to take me down. Exhaustion starts to conquer my fear. *Come on, where are Feldman and Dan?!* It's scary how slowly time is crawling by. I feel like I've been kneeling here outside the car for half an hour.

Suddenly, I spot a red dot, potentially a laser sight from a sniper rifle, flickering on a nearby building. I raise my weapon, prop my elbow on my knee, and stare through the crosshairs toward the direction of the laser. My whole body tenses up as my heart pumps adrenaline, instantly dispelling my exhaustion. The red dot is still flickering across the building wreckage. I wonder whether to sim-ply shoot at the building. I think I can spot movement, a shadow moving somewhere in the rubble. *Guy, cool it,* I tell myself. *You're in a kibbutz, there might still be civilians here, and there are definitely other soldiers.* I can't shake the thought that I'm in the middle of a completely destroyed kibbutz, but I still haven't grasped the true scale of the horror that unfolded here. I have a few more minutes' grace until the picture becomes clear.

Dan and Feldman head back, together with a couple — a man and a woman. They get in the Toyota, squished between me and Rafi, and we start driving. The couple had locked themselves in their safe room and held out for twenty-four hours. We speed toward the exit of the kibbutz and arrive at the impromptu evacuation point outside the gate. I help the couple get out and join their neighbors, who are still waiting at the gates for someone to take them away to safety. Reinforcements keep streaming in. I'm milling between soldiers and exhausted civilians sleeping on the ground. I hear sobbing sounds behind one of the bushes. Dan is standing next to the ambulances on standby, engines running in the parking lot. "Right, let's head back in to keep searching," says Feldman.

But now, as the first rays grow into a full-fledged sunrise, there's nothing to hide the view, no cover of night to obscure the scene before us. Dawn reveals a community drenched in blood, casting a merciless spotlight on the wasteland left behind by the murderous rampage of the entire previous day.

Down the kibbutz pathways, I think I make out shadows, dark shapes slithering across the front yards and driveways. The kind of things your imagination can conjure with little effort, after twenty-four hours of nonstop movement, leaving room for doubt as to what you are really seeing. Identifying targets amidst the rubble is particularly difficult when you're focused on other tasks, like scouring for signs of someone who's still alive and in need of help. Gradually, throughout our search, the horrors become clear.

Bodies are everywhere. Women, men, children. Through the rubble of collapsed walls, bodies are sprawled on the bare ground. A severed limb. Bloodstains leading to a man gunned down, clearly in flight. Smack in the middle of the road is the body of a woman face-down on her belly, like a castaway object. We walk past a parked car, and next to it lies a body riddled with bullet holes. Absolutely shredded. There are children's bodies outside their homes.

There is only silence in the vehicle as we slowly roll past the scene of slaughter. I have nothing to say, nothing to think of. We turn down one of the paths between the houses. *How many people were murdered last night? Where do we even begin? Have terrorists managed to overrun every other village in the south?* My cell phone is out of juice. I have no idea what's been going on beyond my immediate bubble since I arrived on base yesterday morning. Utter ruin is everywhere I look, in every direction. Bodies of civilians of all ages are flung by the wayside. Bloodstains congeal on the asphalt.

"It's a disaster on a scale of…" starts Feldman, but he can't complete his sentence, and it just hangs in the air, lingering over us. As we drive through the kibbutz, searching for any survivors who still need help, I feel like I'm in a horror movie. It's as if the most horrific screenplay ever cooked up has hijacked reality. My eyes jump from body to body, some torn apart beyond recognition. Nobody could have imagined something like this ever happening, not in our worst collective nightmares. When you're in the middle of a mission and your brain and body are busy functioning at overdrive, being in denial about the scale of the disaster is a built-in coping mechanism. But now there's nothing left to keep our minds off it, and as we scour for signs of life, we're overwhelmed by the abundance of death all around us.

Whoa, this is like the Holocaust, I think to myself. *The numbers are so massive that I'll never wrap my head around how big it is.* It's like the stories about the Yom Kippur War, when Israel was nearly overrun by Egypt and Syria. Our grandparents talked in hushed tones about how in the first few days, no one could comprehend the magnitude of what happened.

We drive down the perimeter road encircling the kibbutz. At the section facing the Gaza Strip, a tank has mounted a recently constructed dirt heap. As we drive past, it fires a shell. There's Arabic graffiti scrawled across one of the houses. Smoke is billowing out of another. Everything feels so familiar, like I've been here before, although I'm sure I've never stepped foot in Be'eri.

Suddenly, the dime drops: this place reminds me of the houses in the kibbutz I grew up in. My grandpa's house on Kibbutz Ramat Yohanan. I feel like we're driving down the road from my grandpa's house to the communal dining room, like we do when my siblings and I visit him on Fridays. I'm stunned by the thought: that the rubble of that house looks so much like my grandpa's house. Instantly, everything looks so familiar. The body flung by the bike racks looks like a mannequin from the training simulator back at 669's base. The hedgerows with the pink flowers are just like those in my neighbors' front yard, opposite my parents' house. I realize my mind is playing tricks on me. Making everything around me, the whole environment, deceptively familiar—giving me a sense of déjà vu.

My eyes are already half-shut, tears blurring my vision. I'm partially blind right now, and I can't tell if I'm just exhausted or if my soul's trying to protect itself.

HOW COULD WE NOT COME?

October 8th, 2023
17:30
Guy
A gas station at a junction in the Gaza Envelope

"We're okay," the soldier with the blond buzzcut mutters into his phone. "I promise you, sweetie. Everything's okay."

"Sorry, man. It won't be much longer. I was out of battery and couldn't talk for two days," he whispers to me, with a look as if he's begging for more time on my cell phone.

I shrug and say, "You've got all the time in the world."

It's evening. The night is falling. My legs are dead tired, but if I sit down, I'll fall asleep. So, I lean back on the hood of our pickup truck parked at the edge of the gas station forecourt. The convenience store has been completely ransacked, and bullet holes adorn the walls inside behind the gaping broken windows.

The soldier who asked to borrow my phone, to reassure his family that he's still alive, keeps pacing in circles. He clearly doesn't feel comfortable wandering off, as if worried I'll think he's trying to steal it. Even so, he keeps a certain distance for the sake of privacy and whispers, so

I won't hear him calming down his crying girlfriend, or mom, or other hysterical loved one.

After a while, he hands me back my phone. "Bro, thanks a lot. You don't understand how much I appreciate it," he mumbles. I can see on his face the storm raging inside him. How the outside world—thoughts of his family, friends, and girlfriend—has suddenly penetrated the shell of the crazy situation he has found himself in, cut off from his loved ones, for the past thirty-six hours.

"Feel free if you need some more time; I can charge in the Toyota," I reply, pointing at our loyal pickup truck.

"No, man, I'm good." The last thing you could say about him is that he's *good*. What he means to say is that talking on the phone more won't do him any good.

"Good on you for calling," I say, patting him on the shoulder.

"I'm Erez, from Shin-13," he said, using the Shayetet 13 navy commandos' nickname.

"Where'd you get here from?" I ask him, meaning: *what have you all been up to since Saturday?*

"We got flown over from our base. During the flight, our helicopter got hit—I think it took a missile—but we managed to land," he says matter-of-factly, as if telling me about something he had just seen in the news.

"We took part in the fighting in one of the villages, and then we picked up bodies. I trained as a medic, and we were always told you need a paramedic or a doctor to determine death. I swear I don't know why, I just declared so many people dead…" His laugh is hollow; he knows he's just told an unfunny joke.

"But hang on, you said your name is Guy and you're from Unit 669?" he says, furrowing his brow, his trail of thought going somewhere. "Are you the one who wrote that famous book that all the guys read before going into the army?"[15]

"Yup, that's me," I say with a smile, a little embarrassed.

"But what are you doing here?" he asks, astonished. Like I'm a character who just hopped out of the pages of a book. I answer with a shrug.

Still asking myself the same thing.

Earlier today, around noon, I went to sleep for the first time since yesterday morning. Or rather, I passed out cold in our pickup truck because I was so tired. Now, its early evening, and Feldman, Dan, and I are back in the pickup, waiting to link up with another unit. Suddenly, I remember that I've been meaning to send Ron a message. We drove past his kibbutz a couple of hours ago.

What up bro, u alive? I type. Luckily, he texts back immediately.

You've got no idea what I've been through, he replies. *You free in 15 min? I wanna call and tell u.*

I'm about to text him back, but suddenly we hear shouting in Arabic.

"Waqf, waqf—stop!"

The clicking sounds of rifles cocking. A white Citroen veers into the gas station forecourt. Dozens of armed soldiers lunge forward, surrounding it on all sides. Dozens of soldiers, each more jittery than the next. Every single one has run into terrorists over the past two days. Many lost friends because they weren't alert enough. The men in the car leap out, raise their hands above their heads, and when they see that it's not enough, with countless barrels still pointed right at them, they lie down on the asphalt.

---

15 Guy's diary from his five years of service between 2013–2018 was published and became a bestseller and will soon be published in English.

"Strip!" someone hollers at them. His eyes, red with exhaustion, pop out of their sockets. A swarm of soldiers surrounds the vehicle and inadvertently all point raised barrels at one another. "Don't shoot! You're all aiming at each other!" screams the officer with blazing eyes. Meanwhile, as soldiers sweep their vehicle, it turns out that the "suspects" lying on the ground are Israeli citizens.

"This is a closed military zone. How the fuck did you get here? Get the hell out of here!" screeches the soldier with the blazing eyes.

Suddenly my phone rings. My little brother Ari is finally calling me back. I step away from the melee and pick up.

"What's up, bro?" I ask him in a high-pitched voice, clearly stressed. We haven't spoken since Noga dropped him off at Beit Lid, where his unit, Sayeret Nahal, is garrisoned.

"Listen," he says and suddenly stops. Silence, stretching on for a couple of seconds. "It's tough. Really tough." I keep quiet, giving him space, giving him a chance to elaborate, if he wants.

"Soon after I got to the base, we were taken by helicopter to the border area. We had no idea what was going on. Seriously, Guy, nobody prepared us." He stops for a second. "We got to the base, and the atrocities we saw there, Guy…" His voice cracks. I don't make a sound.

"Barnash got killed, a couple of other commanders in my battalion got killed—we've had guys killed and injured on my team too."

Ari got out of the army a couple of months ago. He's applying to college and was meant to fly to Nepal on Saturday, October 7, but because of my dad's medical situation, he canceled his flight.

"Ari, I'm so sorry," I mumble. I know how much he loved and admired Yehonatan Tzor, better known as Barnash, his battalion commander.

"There were bodies everywhere. Bodies of terrorists we managed to take out. Bodies of soldiers. Female soldiers too. The whole base was full of bodies. Pieces of limbs and blood everywhere. They slaughtered them. It took us time to start clearing the bodies because the smell was unbearable at first."

He keeps describing what he saw, explaining how they went from base to base, eliminating terrorists and clearing bodies, and that they would soon be heading out on another mission—to secure the repair of one of the breaches in the fence with Gaza. The breaches through which terrorists were still reportedly filtering in.

It's dark already. I listen to Ari, slowly dragging my legs beneath me and kicking the gravel. The commotion around me fades away. It's like I'm alone in the world. Nothing else exists but my little brother, who was supposed to be landing in Nepal right now and living the dream of a backpacking adventure around the world; the dream of stunning views, of shouting with joy, of hitting on girls at parties. Right now, he should be trying to shake off memories of grueling military service in Jenin, where he served for a year and spent so many nights engaging terrorists in gunfights.

This isn't how it was meant to go. He doesn't deserve this. And now I'm still silent because I can't bring myself to speak. Tears clogging up my throat, tears flooding my eyes. Instead of climbing up to breathtaking horizons in the Himalayas, he's clearing away his friends' bodies. He keeps talking and I wipe away the tears gushing silently down my cheeks.

"What about you?" he asks. I try to tell him, to force the words out of my mouth, but I splutter. Ari catches my drift and takes back the reins, changing the subject.

"You know Dad's having a pacemaker put in today?"

I feel like I have been thrown into another dimension. My sense of time is completely mismatched with reality. Resuscitating my dad feels like a distant dream. I think about my dad and realize parts of my soul have already said goodbye to him, making their peace with the fact that one day, he'll no longer be alive. *Guy, he's alive!* I remind myself. *He's alive and he'll live! And he'll be at your wedding!* I am trying to stop my tears with the power of positive thinking.

Finally, I manage to muster the strength to talk again. "Bro, Georgia—remember we were there once?" I say with a chuckle.

"Whoa! That's exactly what I was thinking. Feels like it's was years ago. But hey, that was fun, wasn't it?" says Ari.

"Especially for Dad," I say sarcastically.

"I meant till Dad…" he mutters. "Come on, you know what I meant," he laughs. Suddenly someone in the distance calls Ari. "Hey man, I've gotta run."

"Look after yourself, Ari, stay safe," I tell him. I have always hated that expression. If you're looking after yourself, you don't join the army. If you want to stay safe, you don't wear a uniform, and you definitely don't run south while the most horrific attack this country has ever known is unfolding in real time. But here we are.

I take a few deep breaths to calm myself down, rubbing my eyes to wipe away the tear stains. Suddenly, I hear voices again, and people shouting, "Stop!" A civilian vehicle veers into the forecourt. Dozens of guns are cocked, pointed at the car.

Out of the vehicle, a new Mercedes SUV steps a family. "Don't shoot!" shouts the father, stepping out of the driver's seat, his hands in the air. "We've brought food for soldiers!"

"How did you get in here?? I'm losing it. Aren't there roadblocks?" bellows the officer with the puffy red eyes, his voice hoarse.

"Yeah, there were roadblocks, sure," says the father in a French accent, adjusting the black kippah on his head. He opens the trunk, revealing dozens of boxes. His daughters start handing them out, passing them over to the hands that were pointing rifles at them till just a minute ago. I can see hummus, pasta, and meat. One of the girls pulls out a bag with what looks like socks and toothbrushes.

"The police blocked the road, they said it was dangerous here," the father says. "So we drove through the field. We've come from Jerusalem. We read online that soldiers were short on food, and we couldn't leave you all hungry," he says straightforwardly, without a trace of irony.

Go figure.

TAKE COVER

October 10th, 2023
08:30
Guy
A road on the outskirts of the town of Ofakim

We've been attached as a squad to another unit, and we're now waiting around on standby. Our mission is to respond to "localized" incidents. That's a fancy way of saying that we're a bunch of twenty-somethings with four Hummers and, of course, our beloved pickup truck and radios. We're all tuned into and listening in on the frequencies of other friendly forces operating in the area. If we hear that someone's coming under fire, or that there are casualties to deal with, we are to drive as quickly as we can in that direction to begin extraction and treatment.

When we linked up with this current unit, we jumped into the usual discovery ritual that happens whenever Israelis or even Jews in general meet. *Do you know so-and-so?* We banter, throwing out the names of other people we know from their unit, past and present. But this time, instead of the typically enthusiastic responses ("*Of course!*" "*What a guy!*" "*No way, you know him too?*"), the answers come through in mournful whispers:

"Looks like he was killed..."

"He's in critical condition in a hospital somewhere..."

Barely an hour later, we've been radioed into action. I was on the phone with Noga when we got the GO command. Since Saturday morning, we've only texted. If I showed our WhatsApps to someone who doesn't know us, they might think we were work colleagues messaging about logistics.

Guy, how do I get a helicopter?

Speak w Alon, sending u his number

Noga, u got a contact for someone in Meginim?

But now that she's calling, I suddenly hear in her voice both a commander on a mission, but also my partner, my fiancée whom I love so much; it courses through my body, calming me down like an extended hug.

So much is happening, and then suddenly, we get an alert over the radio.

"There was shooting in Kibbutz Kissufim. We're being sent in. I love you."

"Look after yourself."

That expression again. I hang up and jump into our pickup truck .

We speed down the road. On both sides of us are cultivated fields, parched soil thirsty for rain at the end of summer. But the first rain of the season is yet to fall, and instead, there are deep ruts crisscrossing the barren fields, the marks left by the heavy tanks. Dozens of war machines are making their way in convoys through the fields, shredding steel treads into the loose soil, heading to the border with Gaza. I am still gripped with fear and a profound sense of loneliness, a sense that everything around me is crumbling. Every building around us might be a terrorist hideout; every passing tractor might contain a Hamas squad.

Along the sides of the road are dozens, perhaps hundreds, of overturned cars, military and civilian alike. They're riddled with bullets from the terrorists who drove past here in the morning just two days ago. What's left of the motorbikes the terrorists rode across border are discarded in a ditch by the roadside. A never-ending trail of death and destruction. I feel myself sinking into despair.

And then, suddenly, the powerful sight of massive steel Merkava tanks, like a herd of galloping war horses, gives me a sense of security. We've taken a hit, a huge one, but we're already up on our feet and preparing for the counter-punch.

We slow down before entering the kibbutz.

We find five casualties, all conscious, with gunshot wounds to their limbs. The terrorists have managed to flee. We load the casualties into cars that will take them to a helicopter, and they set out toward the landing site that Feldman's coordinating with our unit. We stay behind at the gates of the empty kibbutz, a ghost town in more than one sense—but still also a hideout for Hamas terrorists.

"This is only the beginning," says Zsaninski, the commander of the team we have joined. "Far as I'm concerned, there could be a tango hiding behind every tree or building."

We split up into squads and enter the kibbutz on foot. The three of us—Dan, Feldman, and I—walk over to the farm. The pungent smell of chicken poop wafts over from the coops. I tread slowly, as if I'm on a weekend stroll, but my body is tensed up. I didn't need Zsaninski's warning to be on alert. There are so many places around where terrorists could be hiding, it's almost dizzying. Everywhere looks like an ideal place to hide and open fire on soldiers. A predator drone circles in the sky above us, also scanning the terrain.

We're close to the chicken coops. Smoke is billowing out of them. The strong smell of burned plastic blends into the stench of bird droppings, a reminder of the battle with terrorists that raged here earlier.

"Report from the drone," says Dan abruptly. We stop in our tracks. Dan holds the radio to his ear, furrowing his brow, trying to follow the conversation. I pace around nervously, drumming my fingers on my gun. Feldman signals to me to perform a sweep of our surroundings. And to not catch Dan's eye.

Suddenly, we hear gunshots, intense automatic fire. I tense up and raise my rifle, my pent-up tiredness making me jumpy. "It's an attack helicopter," says Dan, his ear still glued to his radio device. "It's reporting it's taken out a tango." He relays what is happening like it's a soccer game.

"Come on," snaps Feldman. The bright sky is covered with clouds, and the sun has changed its hue with the sunset in the west. My radio battery has died. I try to get a sense of what's happening around me. According to the news, this kibbutz and the adjacent Kissufim army base were the scenes of intense fighting on Saturday. And right now, we don't even properly know how intense it really was. After the IDF retook the kibbutz and the nearby base, the terrorists managed to ambush a Golani force performing sweeps in the empty houses. We already managed to evacuate the wounded soldiers there, and the attack helicopter has just taken out one terrorist, but we keep sweeping the scene—there could be more terrorists at large. Or maybe there aren't. Nobody has a clue.

It's possible that a few steps away from us, behind some bushes, are dozens of bloodthirsty jihadists. We just received a report that soldiers might have found a tunnel shaft, but even that's not certain. Nobody knows anything. Besides the whirring of the drones overhead, everything around us seems so quiet, almost pastoral.

We complete our patrol around the barn and the chicken coop, walking toward the gates of the kibbutz. Our brains are telling our bodies to be alert and ready for action, but exhaustion is making it tough. Our bodies just want to rest already. It's been three days of madness and insanity. We've been laying ambushes for terrorists still pouring in from Gaza, and driving like lunatics from one place to the next in the border area, wherever enemy combatants pop up. Incredible tension washes through my body, slowly overcoming my defenses. The pastoral views and warm weather aren't helping my losing battle against exhaustion either. We head back to the Hummer, parked at the kibbutz entrance, and I'm suddenly struck by longing for Noga.

> *Still looking for terrorists in Kissufim.*
> *Dead tired. U?*

"*Red Alert! Red Alert! Red A—*" rings a metallic female voice, and before it can complete the word, a massive explosion makes the ground shake. A pillar of dust rises out of the woods near the road.

Dan, Feldman, and I throw ourselves down on the ground, covering our heads with our hands, as people scream, "*Get down!*" all around us. The first explosion is followed by several loud bangs—mortars crash on both sides of the road.

We wait a few minutes, then stand up and shake the dust off our uniforms. "Everyone check there are no injuries among your men!" shouts Zsaninski.

"Six-six-nine's okay!" Dan reports over the radio.

"I can't believe people actually live like this," says Feldman. "Just a couple of seconds' warning. If you can't take cover, you're dead. What a nightmare."

There's a mobility scooter by the roadside, as if someone—an old man or woman, a senior citizen, I guess—abandoned it there. Or perhaps they were forced to abandon it. Seeing the small electric vehicle next to a convoy of Hummers gives rise to a wry smile. There's a blue sticker on the mobility scooter's handlebar: *LOYAL TO THE DECLARATION OF INDEPENDENCE*. It's a slogan of the anti-government protests that had rocked Israel over the past year.

I sit inside and watch the scene around me. I'm feeling cynical. *Maybe it's all of our fancy defensive systems, our early warning capabilities and rocket interceptors, the whole Iron Dome System and other cutting-edge technologies, that brought us to this moment,* I think. *Because if we didn't have them, we'd never have been able to live for years under constant rocket and mortar fire from Gaza.*

Suddenly, there's a sharp burst of gunfire from right next to us.

"Guys, it's Kalashnikov fire! Terrorists at close range!" shouts Zsaninski.

DON'T SIT DOWN

October 10th, 2023
12:30
Noga
A public bomb shelter in the town of
Sderot, southern Israel

A few hours earlier, Noga had found herself in a public shelter in the deserted town of Sderot, just eight miles from the Gaza border.

A massive explosion shakes the thick walls of the room.

"What the hell, what was that?" blurts Orit in a panic, not expecting an answer though she's speaking for all twenty people sitting around in the small, airless room. The blast was so powerful that it felt like the rocket had exploded right above them or outside at the entrance of their reappropriated communal bomb shelter.

Noga had her phone propped on its charger, but the explosion sent it crashing to the ground. She quickly picks it up and taps the screen, bringing it to life. She checks it is still working after the fall. Without her personal cell phone, she has no way of communicating with the outside world, and she's running a whole battalion from her old phone. For months, she has been putting off buying a new one. She just finished her law degree, but her first paycheck after an exhausting month's work as a trainee at the Supreme Court was less than the cost of a new iPhone and the monthly rent, so she ended up postponing the acquisition.

She breathes a sigh of relief—her phone is still responsive.

"Orit, where's that Border Police force now?" she asks one of the operations officers.

"They've just reached Kerem Shalom," she answers.

"So please move their location on the map," she asks her, doing her best to keep a lid on the anger in her voice. She knows that Orit is tired. Everyone's exhausted. It's been three sleepless days, moving around from place to place. Now they've finally found a protected place to stay, but it's stifling and crowded. Whenever someone goes to the toilet, everyone has to smell it; there are no air vents to carry away the stench.

Since Hamas has been able to steal radios, army computers, and even soldiers' cell phones, Noga is commanding the operations of an entire battalion, previously touted as an exemplar of high-tech multidimensional warfare, like it's the 1948 War of Independence. The real-time locations of all the battalion's forces are marked out with stickers; Orit's in charge of moving them around a satellite map of the area pinned to the wall. There are no comms systems, so all of their communications are currently being conducted through WhatsApp direct messages. They're assuming that by now, the terrorists have probably already compromised the WhatsApp groups using stolen phones.

Both Noga and Ma'or are the commanding officers of a battalion-level Combat Operations HQ. Ma'or served as a company commander in the battalion, and all other commanders of such Combat HQ's brass were previous company commanders or deputy battalion commanders. Noga is a special case: the former commander of the Paratroopers' Reconnaissance Battalion personally invited her to take on the role alongside Ma'or, making her the only woman in the Israeli army in such a position. Their drills for wartime, practiced for years, have simulated commanding the overall operations and activities of their battalion in alternating twelve-hour shifts.

Despite years of regular training, reality threw a wrench into the gears: Ma'or had gone out to fight with the battalion hours before, leaving Noga to head the command-and-control center practically alone. Without someone to share the role with, she has practically no chance to breathe or eat, not to mention sleep. Initially, Noga was angry at Ma'or for grabbing his gun and running into battle instead of doing his designated job back here, and she was anxious too; Ma'or's older and far more experienced in planning, executing, and managing battle operations. But now, three days in, her concerns have faded away. She's commanding the battalion like a natural, and with iron discipline. And when you're suspended between exhaustion and adrenaline-fueled mania, there's no room for second-guessing yourself.

Suddenly, someone knocks on the bomb shelter door. One of the guys walks over to open it and finds two soldiers in the doorway. "The rocket that just landed hit a car, any chance it belongs to someone here?"

Noga's only half-listening, going over the written orders they have just received from the brigade. *Hang on.* She's the only one who arrived in her own car—all the other soldiers left theirs at the base. That's the privilege you get if you're a commander, or if you're the first one on the scene.

"Could be my car," she says, without looking up, then finishes poring over the document and turns to leave the rocket shelter. On her way out, she yanks her phone out of the charger and takes it with her. The air outside is warm. It's the afternoon. They're in a small neighborhood park; there are two slides, some swings, and snack wrappers spilling out of an overflowing trash can—a sign of soldiers in the streets and a lack of utility workers, because aside from the army, the city is completely abandoned. Everyone's been evacuated. She glances at her car—it's unharmed. The car that got hit is the white car parked behind hers. The rocket scored a direct hit, sending smoke billowing out of the front. She notices a scratch along the front door on her car, on the driver's side, probably from a piece of shrapnel. Apart from that, her car, miraculously, is unscathed.

She heads back to the rocket shelter but lingers for a little longer, wanting to grab another few seconds of fresh air. Her legs hurt from standing up for so long. She won't let herself sit down in case she falls asleep. She hasn't taken her shoes off since Saturday morning. *Man, what she'd do for a shower.* It doesn't even have to be a hot one. Just rinsing herself under a faucet would do the trick.

She takes a tired glance at her phone screen. Three hundred messages. Friends, parents, relatives...everyone sending worried messages, because she hasn't been answering. She has no time to answer anyone who isn't a brigade commander. Anyone except for Guy. When she gets a few seconds—when her attention isn't consumed with military affairs—she thinks about him. She's worried about him. As soon as she reached the base on Saturday morning and started to comprehend the magnitude of what was going on, she was hoping against hope that he wouldn't be called up. He was, of course—and he was sent south immediately.

Over the course of the past three days, she's started to understand, along with the whole army, just how bad the situation really is. The more horrific the surprise assault turns out to have been, the more worried she becomes for Guy. She sends him a voice message every couple of hours. He answers her a couple of hours later. Each sign of life calms her nerves, at least temporarily, and she breathes another sigh of relief. His voice gives her strength. She holds onto it for dear life.

Noga keeps thinking about Guy, wondering where he is. She misses him. She calls him. *Come on, pick up…come on…*

"*Hi my love.*"

"Sweetheart! Where are you?" she asks him, and without noticing, squats down on the curb.

"*I dunno, outside some gas station. We're part of a backup team.*"

"Where's the gas station?" she asks. She knows what's happening everywhere in the area. Or, at least, she knows as much as the IDF.

"*We're near Urim,*" he says. It sounds like he's eating something.

"Wow, my love, I miss you so much…" she sighs.

"*I miss you too, Nogi,*" he says, taking another bite. "*Are you taking care of yourself?*"

"Yeah, more or less. It's tough not having Ma'or here. But I get it. He's a paratrooper before anything else. That's who these guys are, they run toward the fire and fight."

"*Right, but he's got a job,*" he snaps. "*What do I care what he wants? He's supposed to take command, to let you rest and catch your breath. Otherwise, how are you meant to do your job?*"

"Honestly, I'm fine. We're doing good work here, promise," she replies. She knows that this is just his way of showing his love, of caring for her and expressing anger that she's not been looking after herself. She wants to tell him about everything she's been through over the past few days. How she stopped an attack helicopter from accidentally gunning down a group of soldiers at the last minute. How she's been managing operations to track down hostages near the border fence.

She wants to tell him about how hard it is, but still, how she's managed to keep calm and stay professional—even when other folks at her headquarters have totally lost it. The person in charge of communications got the news that his best friend was killed at the Nova music festival, and he was undone. Ayelet, responsible for intelligence, left abruptly for her sister's funeral. Noga wants to tell him everything, but more than anything, she wants to know that he's okay.

"The other night, some people came here from Jerusalem; they brought us so much food," he says, nibbling her ear through the phone line. And then—the insufferable beeping of incoming phone calls. The brigade is at war.

Through the phone, she hears someone shouting.

"What's going on there?" she asks.

"There was shooting in Kibbutz Kissufim. We're being sent in. I love you."

"Look after yourself," she says, and then hangs up and gets back on her feet. She turns to head back to the bomb shelter. Her phone won't stop ringing. All at once, she feels a terrible tiredness washing over her, and starts feeling incredibly weak.

Noga walks down the steps back into the shelter. The suffocating stench hits her again, but she knows she'll get used to it in a couple of minutes. She understands that she has no choice anymore: she has to lie down for a bit, or she'll crash. And Murphy's Law says it will happen exactly during a major incident that requires her maxi-mum attention to run things as well as she can.

"Orit, listen a sec," she says, placing a hand on the sol-dier's shoulder. "I'm lying down on the mattress for a little bit." She points at one of the mattresses in the corner of the room. "If anything happens, wake me up. But I've got to crash out a second." She is back in army lingo mode. In three days she's gone back to talking like an IDF officer: you don't *sleep*, you don't *rest*—you "crash out."

"Of course, I'll only wake you up if we really need you."

"Thanks, babe," Noga says, and she means it.

She lies down on the mattress, placing an arm under her head as a pillow and curling her knees under her other arm. Her hair still bears the faint smell of shampoo, a vague reminder of the shower she took on Friday night. That feels like it was years ago. Her eyes close.

Suddenly, she wakes up in a panic and jumps to her feet. She's frazzled, unsure if she had a bad dream or if some-thing urgent pierced her slumber. From the clock, she sees she's been asleep for five hours, but it feels like it's been several days on end.

"What happened?" she says in a loud voice—too loud—staring at Orit. Everyone in the room stops what they are doing and looks at her, confused. "What'd they just say on the radio?"

"Reports of an incident on Kissufim. There are casu-alties, but it's not in our sector. It's got nothing to do with us," says Orit, looking puzzled, not understanding Noga's panic.

"Where? Where's the incident?" she presses her, afraid she heard the radio right, and that the nightmare, that terrible nightmare, was all too real.

HE'LL ALWAYS BE THEIR FRIEND

October 10th, 2023
17:30
Guy
Kissufim

We speed into the kibbutz in our vehicles and reach the casualties. I jump out of the car. There's a soldier sprawled on the ground in front of me—still wearing his vest—and one of his teammates is leaning over him.

"Guy, he took a bullet to the chest and managed to neutralize the terrorist before losing consciousness. He's yours now!" one of the casualty's teammates shouts at me. I grab the injured soldier. His limp body is very heavy. He's a big man, tall and broad-shouldered. I thrust an arm under his back, between his shoulder blades. With my other arm, I cup both his legs and, with a single motion, carry him behind our vehicle. He's cradled to my chest, a macabre version of the romantic way men carry women around in the movies. His head dangles as I haul him in my arms like a massive sack. I take large strides toward the sidewalk, where I put him down and then kneel over him.

He has curly black hair and his eyes are half-open. I notice that he has an injury next to his mouth, a deep cut—though it's unclear what caused it. His breaths are fast and shallow, as if something is stopping his chest from expanding and taking deeper breaths. Then, I notice the red hole under his armpit that looks like a gunshot wound. It's in the exposed area between the front and back plates of his ceramic vest. "Strip him down quickly," I tell one of the soldiers, while considering how to proceed with his treatment. He has a serious injury to his chest that needs to be taken care of, and he also needs to be ventilated. The dude's not breathing.

Guy, look, he's got an entry wound on his side, I tell myself and stick a needle through his ribs on his right, aiming to drain the air trapped between his lungs and his chest. That might be what's stopping him from breathing now.

"Good stuff!" I mutter under my breath, seeing his exposed chest start to rise and fall more significantly—a minor improvement in his breathing. That's encouraging. But not for long.

Feldman and Dan help me treat the soldier. Having stripped him, they flip him over and place him on a stretcher. I quickly examine him and don't see any sign of other injuries. I fumble to try to find a pulse under his palm but feel nothing. The device I've placed on his hand isn't registering oxygen saturation or a heartbeat.

"When's the evacuation?" I shout. "He needs blood transfusions. We've got to get him to a helicopter." Nobody answers me. Everyone is busy treating the many other casualties. Zazsinski signals to me calmly that he will update me soon, as he speaks into his radio.

I hear no answer to my question, understanding that I've got another minute or two on the ground. I quickly insert a tube into his trachea to ventilate him. I feel no resistance while I'm shoving in the plastic tube; that's not a good sign.

I tie the tube to the face to make sure it's not pulled out by mistake and ask again, not cutting him any slack.

"How long we've got?" I shout again, louder. I need to know in order to decide how to continue treating him. Whatever happens, I'm sure he's suffering from an internal hemorrhage. The pulse in his neck is weak.

"Two minutes," he shouts back.

"Get a chest drain out," I ask Feldman. The needle I used is a temporary solution. What he needs is proper drainage of his chest.

I look around his armpit area, searching for the spot to insert the plastic tube—between his fourth and fifth ribs, according to the textbook but, in reality, it's easier to find where the hair stops growing under the armpit.

"Ready with the drain!" Feldman announces.

"Great," I say, glancing back, looking for a pair of hands to take over the ventilation.

And exactly at that point, an update comes over the radio. *"We've got a chopper on the way. Let's move!"*

I hesitate. What do I do? I've got the ventilation tube in one hand, squeezing it every couple of seconds to keep the injured soldier breathing. Feldman is already holding the scalpel and is ready to hand it over once someone replaces me on ventilation. But I'm just a paramedic, halfway through med school, and definitely not a chest surgeon. If I proceed, this is going to take a few minutes. I can demand that they wait with the evacuation, but that will come at a price too. This wounded soldier needs blood, and from the commotion around us, it's clear there are many other casualties who need to be evacuated ASAP.

Feldman's holding the knife out, staring at me and waiting for me to tell him what to do.

I decide to go ahead with an intermediate approach. Feldman gives me the scalpel and I cut into the soldier's armpit, slicing into his skin to expose a thin layer of muscle and then another of fat. I shove a finger into the incision and forcefully jab into the membrane. It makes a popping sound, like a cork being pulled out of a wine bottle, and I immediately hear the fizzing sound of trapped air draining out of the incision. I'm basically performing a temporary drainage of his chest cavity until I have the chance to wriggle the plastic tube in.

When I first heard the trapped air rushing out, it was encouraging, but then I go pale. Gushing through the cut is a huge amount of blood. That's a really bad sign: it means he's also bleeding internally from the chest.

"*Yalla*, let's get outta here!" I tell Feldman, raising the stretcher and running over to the Hummer. We load the stretcher into the Hummer and jump in after it. I sit in the back seat.

"Step on it!" Feldman shouts to the guys up front. The driver has already yanked the gear shift into reverse to perform a rapid U-turn toward the road, but then we hear someone shouting next to the Hummer.

"There's no room in the other vehicles!" they yell, and load another casualty inside.

"What's his deal?" I ask.

"Gunshot to the head," someone answers.

The driver puts his foot down, the roar of the engine deafening us. From a quick glance, the injured soldier is conscious, his face writhing in pain. In an attempt to wrap up the procedure, I ask Feldman to open up the drainage kit, but with the sharp turn on the road and the wide potholes, he nearly flies out of the car. The soldier up front is driving like he's possessed. Two of his buddies are lying in the back seat, injured. Sitting next to me, Dan is talking into his radio.

The injured soldier's chest has stopped rising. He's not breathing at all. I shove my finger again into the incision in his chest—maybe it'll help to drain him again—but only fresh blood comes out. His face is extremely pale. I can't feel a pulse on his neck anymore. In my heart, I already know this isn't going well.

"What's your name?" I say, leaning over the second casualty, the soldier with the gunshot wound to his head. He's still conscious, curled up like a fetus.

"Tamir," he mumbles, grinding his teeth.

"How do you feel?"

His head is bandaged up. His uniform has been cut off, the hairs on his spindly body standing on end. I cover him with a thin blanket. I have nothing else to warm him up with. I tuck its fringes under his body, as it's threatening to fly off in the ferocious wind. "I'm okay. Just hurts. I'm cold," he struggles to whisper. I give him a lollipop with a painkiller.

I decide to stick with Tamir. Resting a hand on his shoulder, I try to shield him from the wind. I lean over him, checking on the soldier who's being ventilated. I shove my finger again into the incision under his armpit — more air comes out, and loads of blood.

"Tell me," Tamir calls out, and I press my ear to his mouth. I can feel my phone vibrating in my pocket. He continues, "Can you get the bullet out of my head? It hurts," he begs feebly. "Can you get it out please?" His eyes are closed. As if trying not to see what is happening around him.

"I'm with you, dude. We'll get you to a hospital, they'll be able to take it out there. We're on our way," I say, trying to get my body as close to his, to warm him up a little. I pull the lollipop out of his mouth. It has done its job, and I want him to be conscious so I can better assess if his situation deteriorates. Too much fentanyl, the painkilling substance in the lollipop, and he could fall asleep for good.

"We're in!" announces Dan, who has been liaising with the 669's rescue team in the helicopter on its way. We stop just outside a cultivated field. Three hundred feet ahead of us, two tanks speed past, followed immediately by the sound of loud explosions. We lower the stretchers and hold them tight next to the vehicles.

I turn my attention again to the seriously injured soldier. I notice the dog tag dangling off his neck. I turn it around to check his name. There are no signs of a breath anymore; no pulse. I get ready for one last medical intervention, knowing that the chances of changing anything are close to zero.

"Guys," I call out to his teammates who were sitting up front, now standing behind me and watching what I am doing, "we're getting on with the treatment." I say it quietly, almost apologetically. But they don't move, refusing to step away from their friend. I see the worry and horror in their eyes, but I refuse to back down.

"I'm asking you, please—go be with Tamir. Keep him talking and call me if he stops." For me, this man is a seriously injured soldier, or maybe already a dead body, lying naked on the stretcher in the open air. That's how I'll always remember him. For me, it doesn't matter how this ends. But for them—his teammates—he represents years of shared experiences and laughs, time with his family and maybe his girlfriend too…. In short, he's a friend, a brother-in-arms. Those should be the last memories of him forever.

The IDF Medical Corps has protocols for what to do when you lose vital signs on the battlefield, when to decide to stop trying to resuscitate someone. I'm about to try the final intervention according to protocol. I start making an incision under his other armpit, to insert the drainage tube.

I feel my phone in my pocket vibrating nonstop. I insert the tube, but then suddenly have a thought: maybe someone from the team in the helicopter is trying to make contact. With my other hand, the one not holding the tube, half of which is inside the injured soldier's chest, I pull out my phone. On the screen: *NOGA*.

I freeze. Staring at the screen. My iPhone keeps vibrating in my hand. My heart stops beating. There's only one thought racing through my mind. *Something bad has happened to her.* I feel dizzy, like I'm out of oxygen. My stomach is churning. We can still hear echoes of explosions nearby. Tanks are rolling past. The Hummers behind me and the whole of reality fades away. The world stops turning. It's just me and my phone, and I don't dare answer it.

Her name disappears from the screen. I see eight missed calls. I type her name and the phone starts ringing. This time I pick up.

"Noga, you okay? Something happen?" I say, flustered.

A strangled cry pulses down the line. *"You're alive... you're alive..."* she pants. *"I haven't been able to breathe for half an hour...I heard over the radio reports about casualties and fatalities in Kissufim. I was sure you're..."*

My heart slowly starts beating again. "Noga, I'm okay. I'm okay," I say, reassuring her and myself. My eyes are shut. I try to steady my breathing. "I'm treating casualties at the helipad now. I'm okay, I'm—" I try to say something reassuring, something nice or funny. But I've got a lump in my throat. I look up at the sky, choking on my tears. Stopping them from bursting out. I can't afford to cry right now.

"I'll get back to you as soon as we're done here," I mutter, struggling to get the words out. "I love you." I hang up and put my phone back in my pocket, as if nothing happened. I try to get back to my work, putting the tube in his chest and stitching the skin around it. But my hands are shaking, and I feel like I'm drowning in a storm far out at sea. It's hard to breathe. I feel like two worlds have collided and exploded, two worlds inside of me. My head isn't even here in the field, although my body is next to the corpse that I'm still insisting on calling an injured soldier.

With great difficulty, I wrap up the medical procedure, and only then do I tell Feldman, completely downcast, "That's it. Let's stop trying." He nods, as if thanking me — thanking me for letting him step away from the body. I can see that he's wondering: *what am I supposed to do now?*

"Check how the other casualty is doing, please," I say, trying to help him out. I'm giving him the off-ramp to walk away.

I find a black jacket in the back of the Hummer. Just an ordinary civilian jacket, must belong to one of the guys. Without asking for anyone's permission, I cover the body, at least as much as I can; the sleeves are extended and cover his face and groin, giving the dead body a modicum of dignity. As if it made a difference to him.

"How are you?" I ask Tamir, the casualty who's still alive. I know that he is okay, but I walk over to draw some strength from him for myself. He nods. He's still curled up like a fetus. His eyes are shut, the wrinkles around them signaling that he's closing them tight, waiting for me to tell him that I've taken the bullet out of his head, to give him the all-clear. I rest a hand on his back and stroke it gently.

"Chopper's here!" Dan announces. The whirring of the rotor approaches from across the horizon, and the beast speeds into view. "Two days ago, a helicopter was hit right here, we've got to be quick," he adds. Struggling, I clamber to my feet.

"Grab the stretcher!" I call out to the others. "Tamir goes in first," I add, pointing at him. He's still conscious.

The helicopter lands a few dozen feet away from us. We sprint over with the stretcher, leaping over the furrows in the field. Our feet stumble over the mounds of earth. The soldiers and medical team are already waiting for us at the hatch of the Black Hawk helicopter. They load the two stretchers on board.

I grab the doctor by the lapel as she leans forward, her head poking out of the hatch. "Gunshot to the chest, no vital signs. The other one took a bullet to the head, still conscious," I manage to shout into her ear. The mechanic gestures frantically at me to step away, slamming the door shut—and off they go into the cloudless sky.

Silence prevails for a moment. I close my eyes, and I hear Noga's stifled cry screaming in my head, banging on the inside of my skull like a drum.

THERE'S NO PLACE LIKE GRANDMA'S

Three months later
Thursday, December 20th, 2023
Guy and Noga
A small agriculture community, Gaza Envelope

"How's it look on me?" asks Noga, glancing at me through the mirror on the wall. She has just taken off her olive uniform and is in the process of throwing on a short white dress instead. Her slender shoulders slope down to her freckled back. She tugs the hemline of her dress and wriggles her hips from side to side, like she's warming up on the dance floor.

"Nogi, it's amazing," I say, and I really mean it, staring in awe at the delicate white fabric hugging the silhouette of her body. "So, is this the dress for the wedding ceremony?" I ask naively.

She spins around and stares at me in shock. "Are you serious?! It's the dress for the party. What's wrong with you? You won't see the dress for the ceremony until the day itself."

I shrug. If it were up to me, I'd rock up to my own wedding in jeans and flip-flops. You know what? I could even do sneakers. They're more comfortable to dance in.

It's late afternoon in one of the now-evacuated villages near the Gaza Strip. The kindly old grandma who lives in this apartment, probably since she moved to Israel in the 1950s, has gone off to live with one of her daughters. In her absence, the house has become accommodation for trooops. And for a short while until Noga has to go back to her shift, to let Ma'or go get some sleep. The living room of this tiny home, still covered in photos of grand-kids, has become a bridal parlor out of some sort of weird Cinderella story.

Noga has been living here for nearly three months, sleeping on a mattress in the living room together with who knows how many other soldiers from the Paratroopers Brigade. Their Operational HQ is located in the nearby base. From time to time, she has to pop into the Gaza Strip, but she only tells me once she is safely back. Like I could stop her if I tried.

The reason for this quick visit, apart from how des-perately we miss each other, is because we haven't seen each other in several weeks and the bride-to-be needs to try on outfits for the upcoming big day. Like a courier, I have brought her a box of shoes and a dress wrapped in nylon. "Where are the shoes from?" I ask, as she tries on a pair of white heels.

"I asked one of my soldiers to help me and she found them online."

"You mean you gave a subordinate an order to pick out wedding shoes for you?" I say dramatically, pretending to be horrified. "Are you sure that's according to proce-dures?" She rolls her eyes. I walk up and press myself against her from behind. I wrap my arms around her waist. "Maybe in this elderly lady's house, there's a room that's a bit more private…?" I ask. She shoots me a cheeky glare.

It's two months until our wedding. Every day, we wrestle with the decision of whether to postpone. We're constantly going back and forth, trying to prophesize when the army will let reservists go home and the war will be over. Should we stick to the original plan or surrender to a new reality and wait for more peaceful days? Or should we at least wait for a time when both bride and groom aren't still mobilized for emergency reserve duty?

We chose and announced our wedding date, the Jewish holiday of Tu B'Shvat, half a year ago. It is the Jewish new year for trees, a holiday celebrating renewal and flourishing. One of the reasons we chose the wedding hall at Kibbutz Shefayim is that family and friends coming in from abroad would be able to stay at the kibbutz's hotel, located just a short walk from the dance floor. But by this point, many previously confirmed guests announced that they couldn't attend because of the situation in Israel. Many of our other friends are doing reserves and say that the chances of managing to get out for the night are slim. The Home Front Command, which keeps changing its guidelines for public gatherings on a daily or even hourly basis, could force us to cancel the event the day before. Everyone we know who was supposed to get married in the next six months has already postponed their wedding until further notice. And now, despite the expectations we built up, the war is only getting more intense and seems far from winding down. One of my army buddies put it well after I explained our dilemma to him: "I know you want to get married, but I still don't get the big rush to do it now. I personally wouldn't be ready to gamble with the most important and expensive night of my life."

The day after Noga tried on dresses with me at the old lady's house, I headed back to Tel Nof Airbase to be on standby for the Sea Stallion helicopter's rescue team. In the evening, I call my dad to check how he is doing. "I was with your mom at a doctor's check-up today," he tells me. "The doctor says the pacemaker's working, everything looks fine."

"And how do you feel?"

"Your mom, Eden, and Sivan are taking care of me. I'm still weak but getting stronger day by day." In the distance, I hear an announcement over the loudspeaker. I try to concentrate on my dad's voice; it sounds so faint over the phone. "I got out today for a short walk. Every day, I manage to walk a little farther," he adds.

"I'm really happy to hear that, Dad. You really can't take it for granted!" I tell him, and that happiness is sincere. I sit down on a bench in the middle of the base, near the fitness center. "Honestly, well done!" A bunch of trainee soldiers walk out of the nearby 669 fitness center, strolling casually, despite wearing vests with heavy weights to make their training extra hard.

"Guy, you coming to the briefing in the HQ?" I hear a voice behind me ask. I turn around. Hannah, the doctor on our standby team, walks past me. I gesture to her with a swivel of my hand, as if to ask, *What's up?* "Dunno," she says, "they said over the loudspeaker, everyone on base should head to the Ops room." I signal to her that I'm on the phone and will join soon.

"Guy, can you hear me?" my dad asks.

"Yeah, I'm with you." I refocus my mind on the conversation. I tell him about visiting Noga, and I can tell that hearing about the wedding preparations makes him happy. When I told him a few weeks ago that we were thinking of postponing the wedding, he reacted in a way that made me fear his heart would stop functioning properly.

"Did she let you see the wedding dress?" he asks in amazement.

"What d'you think? Of course not." I tell him off just as I got told off. "It was just the dress for the party afterward." A few minutes later, Hannah and the others — rescue soldiers and the logistical support teams — head out of the main headquarters. They disperse, all walking in silence. Something seems off.

"Dad, I've gotta go, let me get back to you."

"Don't forget to call tomorrow and receive a blessing before Shabbat," he adds and hangs up. I walk up to one of the guys. He looks agitated.

"What happened?"

"Shai Ayeli was killed," he says quietly.

It's nearly three months into the war. Unit 669's teams are everywhere. They are attached to brigades deployed inside Gaza, waiting to be sent into action at a moment's notice, on standby along the border, and, in case of an incident with casualties, ready to navigate their way at lightning speed through the most complex areas to extract wounded soldiers. And of course, the Black Hawk and Sea Stallion helicopter teams are in the rear on standby on Air Force bases.

As soon as there is a report of a casualty, 669's well-oiled machine springs into action. I say well-oiled, because it executes as many as dozens of missions every single day. The unit swoops into the Gaza Strip and loads casualties into vehicles packed with the unit's soldiers, paramedics, and doctors, who then start to administer treatment on the move — and frequently under fire. Giving them advanced medical care while driving at a million miles per hour, in total secrecy, and coordinating with a helicopter already circling in the air as to where to meet them. The helicopter lands and, in no time at all — often just a matter of seconds—the injured soldier is manhandled into the cabin and handed over to other 669 team on board.

These missions run smoother and smoother as the war drags on. This well-oiled machine includes many support cogs you don't see on the frontlines. The whole operation brings together drivers and quartermasters, and cooks and armorers, working nonstop, around the clock, so that the teams on the frontlines have everything they need. It brings together 669 officers at the command center and Air Force HQ planning these sorties and preparations for rescue missions. It brings together soldiers stationed at the underground command node at the Air Force HQ with various divisions, sitting next to operations managers and feeding them information from the field, helping them make decisions at the critical and chaotic moments when things go wrong—which is exactly when a rescue team needs to be sent in.

But notwithstanding all of our evacuations, rescue missions, and extractions under fire, the war is claiming a heavy and mounting human toll.

The last time I saw Ido Yehoshua a few months ago, at a training exercise, he told me that he and his wife, Ziv, were about to become parents. He was killed in a gunfight with terrorists on October 7th. Dr. Eitan Naaman, a pediatric ICU specialist who only recently joined our unit, was also killed in battle. Ben Shelly, fresh in his role as a company commander in 669, was killed in combat in the Shejaiya neighborhood in Gaza alongside Rom Hecht, a young rescue soldier who had just finished his training a couple of months earlier. They were killed during an attempt to rescue soldiers who were shot. David "Dudi" Digmi, a paramedic, fell after returning from Active duty in the Gaza Strip. Netanel Eitan—Nati—was killed in action as an officer cadet just before he was meant to enter the role of team leader in the unit. I was an instructor of his team at special forces tryouts, and the representative of 669 to try and scout candidates to begin the pipeline. At the end of the grueling tryouts, there are personal interviews; while others in his group talked largely about how they prepared with combat fitness groups and exhausting CrossFit workouts, he spoke modestly about volunteering at hospitals, where he worked to cheer up kids who were sick with cancer. Daniel Alloush and Tom Ish-Shalom, both past the age of service, re-enlisted voluntarily during the war. Killed in a helicopter crash on the way to rescue casualties.

I sit down on a bench and watch Shai's teammates hugging each other and making calls to update their buddies in the unit's various rapid-response teams spread across the country. Between the sniffles and coughing to cover up their tears, I hear snippets of sentences.

"Bro, listen to me for a sec — we lost Shai."

"The funeral's sometime tomorrow. I guess in Ashkelon."

"Crazy how we lost the best goddamn guy on our team, hey?"

I stay there, still staring at them. All of Cohort 49, like a flock roosting at nightfall. They sit together around a picnic table next to the concrete cylinder serving as a bomb shelter in the middle of the base. One of them is slumped forward, his head in his hands, his fingers covering his eyes. His feet are shaking. The soldier next to him has his arm around him, awkwardly patting him on the back. They sit together for a while, and finally the guy with his face in his hands gets up slowly. He pats down his uniform, tucks his shirt into his pants, and says hoarsely, "Come on, we've got a eulogy to write."

I'M ON ANTIBIOTICS

Friday, December 22nd, 2023
09:00
Guy
Unit 669, Tel Nof Airbase

The following day, Cohort 49 is swapped out with operators from other cohorts so that they can go to Shai's funeral. When it ended, they headed back to base; back on call. Back to war.

The sun has already set when a siren begins to shriek. The operations officer calls, *"Wildcats, you're on! Wildcats, you're on!"* through our radios and the loudspeaker system, launching our rapid-response rescue team at Tel Nof into action.

I sprint to the launching room, and the hangar door slams shut behind with a painful screech. Barnea, the rescue team commander, is already there and starts the engine of the car that will carry us across the base to the waiting helicopters. *"Gaza. No details yet,"* crackles a voice over the comms system. Barnea checks everyone is there. "Right, everyone in the cars. Let's go!"

Reflexively, the siren blaring on the base's loudspeaker system makes your body secrete stress hormones, kicking the nervous system into action and driving up your heart rate for what equates to systemic full-throttle.

We quickly load our equipment into the vehicles and speed out through the garage doors toward the road that bisects the base. I get dressed as we drive, trying not to lose my balance every time we hit a speed bump. It's a Friday night, and we race past soldiers strolling back from the synagogue on the base.

The soldier in the driver's seat breaks with a screech a couple of yards behind the tail of the massive Sea Stallion helicopter. The sound of the engines and rotor blades picking up speed is deafening. I stick in a pair of earplugs and leap out of the car. Together with the technicians who are in charge of maintaining this aging helicopter, we load our equipment into the belly of the huge beast. After a few minutes, Barnea gives the pilots the green light, signaling that the whole gang is on board, and that they can take off.

The Sea Stallion accelerates and ascends off into the sky. Meanwhile, we get the cabin ready to take in the wounded soldiers we're racing toward. Given the helicopter's relatively large size, the Sea Stallion team gets dispatched to mass-casualty incidents. As a result, the team always includes three senior medical staff—meaning a doctor and two paramedics. Jonathan, the other paramedic, and I head over to hang our equipment on the walls of the helicopter.

By this stage of the war, we are all battle-hardened. No one is talkative or nervous. I put on my vest, adjust my helmet, and tune into the radio system.

"*Barnea, do you copy?*" asks the captain.

"*Loud and clear.*"

"*There's a firefight in the northern Gaza Strip, and another simultaneous incident in the south.*" The back-and-forth on the comms is wild, and it's hard to get a clear picture of the incident at hand. Other helicopters that are taking off from Palmachim and Hatzerim Airbases are on their way to twin mass-casualty incidents too. To me, it all sounds like acoustic chaos but to the pilots, the grainy radio chatter is their mother tongue.

"For now, we know of six casualties. The Black Hawk helicopters will go in, each chopper will take two casualties and we'll also take two. Got it?"

"Roger that!" Barnea confirms that he heard and understood everything. In every rescue mission, especially in a war, the number of casualties is in constant flux. Until we land, these details have no meaning, as we are about to discover. As they would always tell us during interminable forced marches in basic training, *"You gotta smile at changes of plan."*

"Main: Sheba. Second: Barzilai," says the captain, telling us to which hospitals we are going to evacuate the wounded soldiers. The IDF Medical Corps decides where the casualties go, especially if, like today, there are multiple simultaneous mass-casualty incidents. Today, our assigned hospital is Sheba Medical Center, near Tel Aviv. But if we assess that we have a casualty in critical condition who needs immediate surgery, who might not survive the extra ten minutes in flight, we can always land at Barzilai Medical Center in Ashkelon, which is much closer to Gaza. It doesn't have the same trauma care facilities as Sheba, but sometimes emergency surgery to stop bleeding is preferable to a longer flight to a trauma center.

Over the course of these countless aerial extractions, I'm always shocked by how close the Gaza Strip is to the Tel Aviv metropolitan area.

"Waiting for permission to go in. We're five minutes out," says the pilot, announcing that we've reached the war zone.

The Sea Stallion circles in the air. We're close to the border, as close as we can get to the incident without putting the helicopter in range of Hamas firepower. We wait for a green light from the ground forces, locked and loaded, just waiting for a finger to squeeze the trigger.

It's a nerve-racking wait. I look at my team members, all standing in perfect silence inside the helicopter. Everyone is concentrating on the communications over the radio system, trying to get a sense of what's really happening on the ground, of what we're about to meet as soon as the wheels hit the sandy surface of Gaza.

I've already been on several missions with Jonathan and Hannah, our Doc. Despite being a few years younger than me, Barnea has been my team commander for quite a few special operations. I also carried out another rescue mission with Winnick, an excellent operator, when a Eurocopter AS565 Panther helicopter crashed into the Mediterranean about two years ago. And as for the three other soldiers in our team—Cohort 49, who are still in mandatory service—we haven't done any rescue missions together, but I feel like I know them all well. Last night, I watched them writing a eulogy together for their fallen friend.

"*Copy that, we're going in.*" I hear the other Black Hawk helicopter getting permission to go in. Two minutes later, it's our turn. "*Eagle, this is Wildcats,*" I hear a voice crackling. The Unit 669 soldiers in vehicles on the ground are radioing the pilots, our helicopter.

"*Loud and clear, Wildcats.*"

"*On my way now to Helipad 5865,*" the team's commander says, updating where they want the helicopter to land. "*I've got three casualties. Gunshot wounds. Conscious, on stretchers.*" The pilots get final approval.

"*Barnea, did you catch that?*" the pilot checks.

"*Three casualties, gunshots,*" Barnea confirms. "*We're going in.*"

Like a horse speeding out of the gate at the sound of the starting gun, the helicopter races ahead. The pilot tilts the wheel westward and descends. We all look outside through the windows of the darkened cabin, scouring for threats, scanning for sources of rocket fire toward the helicopter. We're flying completely black—no lights whatsoever—to avoid detection from enemy forces potentially lying in wait below. The ground passes quickly beneath us. Fields, buildings, and whole neighborhoods appear and disappear in the blink of an eye. Suddenly, the helicopter takes a sharp lurch.

"They'll be at your six o'clock," says the pilot, completely focused as he begins the descent for a rapid landing. The mechanics lean out of the ramp, watching the fast-approaching ground under the belly of the Sea Stallion to check that there are no obstacles hiding in the darkness.

In an instant comes a light thud, making the helicopter judder and signaling that the wheels have hit the sand. The bird has landed.

I shift my gun to my side to free up my hands for loading up the casualties. I quickly start to notice that the situation doesn't seem to match the report we received of just three casualties. I count one, two, three, four, five. Five stretchers. I pull the first stretcher, aggressively dragging it along the floor, because it's preventing the other casualties from getting hoisted inside, all in pitch darkness.

The 669 team on the ground carries another stretcher bearing another casualty. I feel a massive thwack on the back of my neck. I look behind me and hear someone shouting in the darkness. "Guy, take good care of them!" I can't work out which member of the ground force just dislocated a vertebra in my neck.

In sixty seconds, the stretchers have all been loaded into the helicopters in what was a perfectly orchestrated process. And then we're off; we all drop down to our knees in order not to lose our balance during the rapid ascent, and to signal to the mechanics that the Unit 669 ground force has disembarked, and only we—the aerial team arriving with the helicopter—are still onboard.

I feel my innards dropping in what is the body's instinctual reaction to a rapid climb in altitude. Gravity glues me to the floor of the helicopter as we take off into the night. I reach out into the darkness, grab the pole of the stretcher, and get back on my knees. I switch on my headlamp and take a quick glance at the two injured soldiers on either side of me. The first thing I notice is the excruciating pain writ large on their faces.

The soldier next to me from Cohort 49—he's also called Guy—is already hooking them up to monitors. I give them a quick physical examination. I need to confirm what injuries they have, and make sure there's no active bleeding.

The mechanic switches on the lights, indicating that we've left the Gaza Strip, flooding the cabin with a dim light. I notice that the injured soldier on the left-hand stretcher looks pale. There is a very deep gash in his left knee. He's lost a lot of blood—despite a tourniquet near his crotch. The other casualty is suffering from shrapnel wounds, small cuts all over his body. I signal to the other Guy to help me flip them over, and I examine their backs and legs.

My mind is racing, as I weigh up how I want to treat them. The other Guy has already hooked them up to an IV. The two soldiers' faces are contorted with pain. They're shivering from the cold. There's no reason for them to suffer like this. I prepare the morphine and ketamine and give them both their first dose. I'm more worried about the one with the deep cut on his leg. A slim young man with black hair, his body is filthy and covered in soot and dust. I can't get a clear read of his blood pressure, but he's unconscious and his heart is racing, which are two indications that he's in shock. There's not enough of a blood supply for the brain to keep conscious and the heart is trying to compensate.

"Guy!" I shout. "We need blood!" He reads my lips and starts preparing a blood transfusion. Dr. Hannah comes up to me, kneels down, looks me in the eye, and gently shakes her head, as if to ask: *what injuries are we dealing with?* I glue my mouth to her ear and shout, "One is conscious and stable, painkillers. The other dude needs blood!" She takes a quick glance at them, nods, and goes back to treating the others.

Cold temperatures are bad for trauma casualties, and the icy wind sweeping through the cabin of the helicopter isn't helping. The two injured soldiers are freezing; I can tell that their teeth are chattering and their bodies are shaking. I cover them both in a thermal blanket. The first strong cocktail of painkillers is helping the one on the right. His face now looks calmer. His pulse has slowed down a bit. I look left. His eyes are closed. I lean next to him and shout into his ear, through the earplugs that the other Guy has popped in: "*What's your name?*"

"Ori," he mumbles. I see his lips move and think that he said, "Ori." From the dog tag around his neck, I see that I guessed right.

"It hurts," he says. His face is still contorted in agony. I give him another dose — the maximum amount, according to the guidelines. The other Guy finishes connecting the blood transfusion to the heating device and looks at me, asking permission to start the procedure. I nod vigorously.

I rest my hand on Ori's shoulder, and with the other, I try again to measure his blood pressure. No dice. His face relaxes. The second dose of drugs is kicking in. He slowly pulls his hand out from under the blanket and reaches out to me, extending an open palm, like he's looking for something. His eyes are still shut. I reach out and he grasps my hand, wrapping his fingers around it in an iron grip. I see that he's mumbling something, and I lean in, next to his ear, trying to hear what he's saying.

"*I can't hear you!*" I shout, my hand still in his palm.

"I'm on antibiotics," he mumbles.

Sometimes the drugs can cause hallucinations; I guess that's the reason why ketamine is in high demand at parties.

"I'm still on antibiotics," he keeps mumbling.

"Everything's okay, we're taking care of you," I reply.

The other Guy keeps pumping him with blood at full force. Nearly done. The device on Ori's finger suddenly shows a pulse. That's a good sign.

Barnea signals that we're five minutes from landing at the hospital. Guy asks me whether he should give the soldier another blood transfusion. I weigh it up but decide that for now there's no need. The helicopter lands with a gentle thud at Sheba Medical Center's helipad. The ambulances are already waiting.

I see the other casualty, the one riddled with shrapnel wounds, lifting his head, as if looking for something. I know what he's looking for. I ask Winnick to bring him his gun. Winnick makes sure his gun is discharged and locked, and I entrust the rifle in the injured soldier's hands. It's an instinct for any soldier, especially a combat soldier, to hold his gun tight. It gives him a sense of security. And in my opinion, if an injured soldier is conscious and capable, he deserves to enter the hospital as a warrior returning from combat, proudly carrying his weapon.

The other Guy grabs the front poles of Ori's stretcher, and I try lifting the back ones, but Ori is still gripping my hand and isn't letting go. I decide that this is part of the treatment, and surrender my hand to his iron grip. I signal to the mechanic to come and help me, one hand still in Ori's grasp, the other holding the pole of the stretcher. We get into the ambulance and drive over to the trauma center. His eyes are still closed. He's still holding my hand, refusing to loosen his grip.

It's a Friday night, and Sheba's medical teams are already waiting by the beds. "From what we know, it was a firefight with hostiles," I tell the doctor on call. We transfer Ori to a hospital bed and the medical staff start plugging him into monitoring devices. Under the glaring neon lights, I get a clear view of the deep injury on his leg. I really hope he'll walk again. But for now, there's nothing more to do. I gently release my hand from his grasp.

"I've got to say, he looks really familiar," says the doctor. I shrug, bundle up the monitor cables, and gather up my equipment so we can go back to the helicopter, to be ready for the next mission. "Hang on," the doctor says suddenly. "Tell me," she says, looking at Ori, leaning over him above the bed, resting a hand on his chest, to grab his attention as the powerful painkillers lull him to sleep. "Haven't you been here already?" she asks, as if she just caught him sneaking into a cinema to watch two movies with one ticket.

He nods slowly. "So that's why I recognize you!" I'm not sure whether she's talking to me or him. Or to herself. "You were wounded. You were here a week ago. A shrapnel wound, if I remember correctly. You're a company commander, right? How the hell did they let you go back into combat so quickly?"

His eyes still shut, his lips curl into a cheeky smile.

"And he's telling me, antibiotics! Over and over. And I can't understand what he wants from me. And then the doctor recognizes him. Turns out he was wounded, and because his soldiers were still inside, he got out, or maybe he just ran away from the hospital," I tell Noga on the phone the following morning. "The guy's a reservist, I saw his address on a sticker at the hospital, he lives near us in Tel Aviv. I really hope he doesn't lose his leg. I swear, what crazy people."

"Totally," she agrees. "Yesterday we had a few incidents in our area, your guys worked hard. It's only thanks to the quick reaction of the recon units' commanders that it ended with only five injured and no dead," she says, before going on to tell me what the Paratroopers Brigade got up to.

Suddenly I hear the operations officer announcing something, and I listen to the loudspeaker, making sure it's not an important announcement. "I'm with you," I tell Noga distractedly.

"What did you say his name was, the company commander who escaped from the hospital and went back to Gaza?" I tell her his surname. "Hang on, hang on," she says slowly, "were you at the incident with the 55th Brigade?"

Sometimes I think the head of the Southern Command doesn't have as firm a grip on the details of the war in Gaza as Noga does.

"No way, I know that guy. We served together a long time. I've got to say, I'm not surprised. What a dude," she adds. "There are many of our battalion hospitalized in Sheba. I think I might go visit them today."

A few hours later, I get a voice note from Noga.

"Hi Guy," says a hoarse voice, "thanks for the ride yesterday, it was really fun, I had a blast the whole journey." In the background, I hear Noga laughing. "I'm on my feet already and joking around with the doctors. Please thank your friends for me too." I shut my eyes and smile to myself.

Is Ori crazy? In a sense, for sure—no doubt about that. *But then*, I think to myself, *This country probably only exists thanks to crazy guys like him.*

MAYBE SOMEDAY I'LL FIND THE WORDS

January 26th, 2024
04:00
Guy and Noga
Shefayim (near Tel Aviv)

The narrow and dreary corridor smells like a basement, reeking of dust and damp and storage. There are bicycles propped up against the wall, mud stains from the tires crisscrossing the gray carpet like confetti, and cardboard boxes full of children's books and board games scattered everywhere. We walk slowly past clothes hanging on drying racks, leaching the sweet aroma of industrial laundry detergent. Children's clothes, sweatshirts. It looks like the staircase of a building where all the tenants have just moved in and haven't yet unpacked. But the inhabitants of these rooms had more than enough time to unpack. In fact, far too much time. They're waiting to return home, although home will never go back to being what it was before.

Noga and I step over the obstacles in silence, holding hands. We stop outside the door of our room. Noga tiredly rummages through the bag slung over my shoulder, looking for the key. "I can't believe this is happening.

That's it, it's behind us," she says quietly, in order not to wake the neighbors.

It is late, but I've never been more awake. "It feels like it's a dream, one that I'm still inside and don't want to wake up from," I reply.

"Let me correct myself. It's not all behind us. It's all still ahead of us," she whispers with a smile, her heart still racing with excitement.

Just a few hours ago, we stood under the wedding canopy. A *tallit*, a Jewish prayer shawl, stretched over our heads, next to our parents, our two brothers, and our two sisters. Rain was pummeling down on the high glass walls of the wedding hall, the smell of ocean air intermingling with desert winds wafting in through the open doors.

When we got to the venue, I noticed curious faces looking out at us from the neighboring hotel. Displaced people who'd been living for far too long in tiny hotel rooms were curious about the first wedding to take place at the venue since the war had broken out. They'd been forced, against their will, out of their homes and had been living in a small hotel since the night between October 7th and 8th. Refugees in their own country. I couldn't meet their gazes — I was terrified that I'd recognize one of the faces from that long, dreadful night.

Later on, surrounded by family and friends, Noga told me just before the ceremony that more than 500 people had showed up. We told the venue to prepare for 300–400 guests, depending on the status of the war. I looked at her. With so many people around us, it still somehow felt like it was just the two of us. Just me and Noga. Standing next to her in a daze, more nervous than I've ever been, I pulled my speech out of my pocket. The words I scribbled on a piece of paper were meant to sanctify our marriage not only according to the law of Moses and Israel,[16] but also by the power of my love for her.

> *Nogi, I need you and your love. I need you more than I can ever admit. I feel like I don't recognize myself without you anymore. You know what's happening inside me and see straight through me. There are times I wake up in the dead of night, my mind racing, thinking about the future, and how we'll make ends meet, and what will happen with this country. And in your sleep, you feel my anxiety and apprehension, and you mumble something soft. You ask me, "Guy, are you OK?" And you remind me everything will be OK, because I have you.*

I pause to breathe for a moment. I feel my father's arm behind me, his hand spread open like a wing, half-touching my shoulder in support. Next to him is my mother, taking occasional, nervous glances at me and Noga and my dad, as if worried his heart can't handle the excitement, trying to protect him with her love. Behind her are my sisters, Eden and Sivan. At the front of the stage is the emcee: Ya'ara, Noga's best friend, who spent a long time plotting the match between us before eventually finding the right moment to introduce us.

And then there's my brother, Ari. Since the start of the war, I've been afraid of looking him straight in the eye, afraid to see the scars left behind by the immense trauma and loss he's experienced. I feel my father's heartbeat through his palm. Thinking about him and Ari, my eyes

---

16   A reference to the Jewish wedding liturgy.

well up. I look up, focusing on the white canopy overhead, take a deep breath, and try to find the strength to
push ahead with my speech.

The cheers and applause from friends and family give
me strength. I look around with a grateful smile. Through
glazed eyes, I see Nana, my maternal grandmother, who
came all the way from Boston to be at my wedding. Next to
her is Noga's Grandpa Shimon, who immigrated to Israel
from Morocco. He's past the age of ninety and still has a
sharper mind than me. Next to him is Grandpa Yonatan,
my dad's dad, a kibbutznik whose parents immigrated to
Israel fleeing persecution in Germany and the steppes of
Ukraine. And I keep reading.

> *And one last thing. When I was rummaging
> through my memories of our moments together, I
> realized how many times I've kicked the can down
> the road, waiting for the right moment to act.
> Waiting to send you a first WhatsApp message
> to ask you out. When we spoke about moving in
> together, I said: let's wait a bit. Even when I thought
> about how and when to propose, I stalled, because I
> wanted to wait for the perfect moment. And now too,
> when we were debating whether to get married under
> the clouds of war, there were days when I thought:
> maybe let's wait, so that all my guys from 669 can
> come and our family abroad can fly in.*

Mid-recitation, I hear the voices of my fellow brothers
from Cohort 42 in Unit 669, who just last night evacuated
casualties and soldiers' bodies out of the ruins of a building in the central Gaza Strip. I hear Noga's friends from
the Operations HQ of the Paratroopers, who haven't been
out of active service in ages other than right now, to go to

their commander's wedding. There's a war on, it's pouring rain and even so, so many people showed up.

> *But today — tonight! — as I hold your hands, I understand already that there's no point wondering whether to wait for the stars to align. Because as long as I wake up in the morning next to you, with my arms around you, holding you close to my heart; and as long as we celebrate the good moments together and in moments of pain, we grieve together; and as long as I have your brilliant almond eyes in front of me, there's no reason to wait, because when you're by my side, and I'm by yours, it will always be the right time. I love you, and I'm still trying to find the words to tell you how much.*

The sun is about to rise, My leg muscles hurt from hours of dancing. I waddled the whole 700 feet, not even that, from the wedding hall to our hotel room. And now, as I pass through the corridor, I reek of sweat and alcohol — my sweat, but also that of all the guests who danced with us into the night. Noga, up ahead of me, smells divine, as always. She pops the key in the lock and slowly opens the door in order not to wake the other guests.

I take one last look behind at the hallway, jammed with objects, a monument to lives disrupted in a heartbeat. Toys and kitchen utensils and photo albums, you name it — anything that didn't fit in a tiny hotel room. After all, this is home to the residents of Kfar Aza, who have been living at the hotel of Kibbutz Shefayim for nearly four months already. People whose whole worlds had been destroyed. They had lost their loved ones, murdered in cold blood, kidnapped to tunnels in Gaza, their homes, their whole lives, and were now living in tiny hotel rooms. The only room not inhabited by residents of Kfar Aza is the one reserved for newlyweds.

"You coming in, sweetie?" Noga whispers, her voice hoarse, already taking off her cocktail dress and flinging off her heels. I nod and linger another moment. I play back the recent, vivid memory of me stepping on the glass under the wedding canopy reciting, *If I forget thee, Jerusalem*, and remembering that happiness in this world will always co-exist with sadness, that there are always fractures in the world that are yet to be fixed. Tonight, of all nights, we find ourselves the guests of Kfar Aza. They live in this hotel, and we're just here for the night. In some sense, they are our hosts, welcoming us under their temporary canopy on our wedding night.

I pause for a moment, allowing the moment to sear itself into my mind, and then step into the room, closing the door behind me.

I quickly undress and get under the blanket, wrapping my arms around Noga's chest. The sound of her breathing slows down my heart, which is still thumping. She gently taps her fingers on my arms.

"I love you. Good night," I say and kiss her head, resting on my shoulder.

"Even today, this is the best moment of the day," she mumbles.

A FEW WORDS FROM
THE AUTHOR

"I never could have imagined something like this happening…"

The words came out in a stutter, under my breath. Almost a week after that black Shabbat, we had stopped to rest for the first time inside one of the ransacked army bases on the Gaza border. The battle-scarred walls, charred and riddled with bullet holes, were still adorned with countless photos of the base's soldiers: young men and women smiling and hugging each other, with little hearts drawn into the corner of each picture. The room had a distinct smell—both the delicate scent of women's perfume and the stench of cigarettes lingered, rising from the floor. Every few minutes, we heard sirens signaling enemy infiltration warnings at other bases or a Code Red that meant incoming rockets. Along with the entire country, we were trying to come to terms with the nightmarish series of events that had unfolded over the past few days. None of us knew where to begin or how to talk about it; how to even verbalize what each of us had experienced. As time passed, and as the unfathomable tragedy of October evolved into full-blown war, I understood even more clearly how hard it was to express any of it in words. I would begin a sentence—"It was…"—but couldn't get much further.

And that's how I came to write this book.

First and foremost, writing it was a form of therapy—a personal attempt to transform this traumatic experience into another chapter of my life. An attempt to use the discipline of writing, which has previously served me so well, to turn the sights and smells of recent months into a thing of the past, rather than letting them remain a kicking, screaming reality that overpowers my daily life. An attempt to turn the pain and anguish into just one story, rather than letting it become the only story in my life.

This book isn't a journalistic account, and it isn't trying to precisely capture events to the minute. It's the true story of a handful of soldiers out of thousands of men and women who dropped everything to rush south. It's an attempt to provide some insight into the story of Unit 669, the IDF's Elite Combat Rescue Unit, one of the four Elite units of the Israeli army, during the October 7th attacks, through the eyes of its members, including those on *kibbutzim* that fought tooth and nail to protect their homes. They are rescue soldiers, officers, and paramedics. The 669 soldiers on compulsory service or reserves who were trained for years to deal with the most complicated situations, and doctors who accompany rescue missions. On helicopters and on the ground, they fought to rescue the wounded from within the battles for the towns and *kibbutzim* of the Gaza Envelope.

But above all else, this is my personal story. Ultimately, I'm just one of millions of Israelis and Jews around the world for whom the personal and the national in the events of October 7th are tightly—almost inextricably—bound together. But the link between the specific and the general doesn't only apply to going through hardship. It's equally true of showing bravery and heroism; of finding the courage to look forward to a brighter future; of having faith that out of the smoldering wreckage of the past, a new, better future may yet bloom.

Guym0to100@gmail.com

ACKNOWLEDGMENTS

This book is the story of many members of Unit 669, a group whose dedication and self-sacrifice know no bounds. A bunch that show up to carry out their duties, often without even being asked, whether saving lives in Israel, or carrying out humanitarian missions across the globe, as has happened multiple times in recent years. Many unit members contributed to the writing of this book, but I can't use their full names — not only for security reasons, but also because they prefer to remain anonymous, and to serve in a spirit of humility and modesty.

I am eternally grateful that I have the privilege to serve alongside them.

Neither this book nor *Full Throttle* (soon to be published in English) would have come to life without the help and support of many people. The entire unit and I owe them immense gratitude — not only for translating Unit 669's story into English, making it accessible to the broader world, but also for their ongoing support of 669 and its soldiers.

Many of the people I'd like to thank specifically requested, with inspiring humility, that I not use their full names, just like the members of the Unit.

Eylon, who with infinite dedication and skill, somehow managed to translate entire books even while being busy translating the spirit of an entire nation to the rest of the world. It's incredible to think that everything started with a quick drink in Rabin Square in Tel Aviv;

StandWithUs, who are so steadfast in advocating for our country across the world—and a special thank you to the incredible **Roz and Sam** for all your support;

Aba and Ima, with love and appreciation for giving me the skills and values to find the first few words, even though reaching the summit makes it easy to forget the initial challenge;

Steven, it will forever be a mystery to me how such an Israeli guy, with such a Sabra heart, was somehow accidentally born in America;

Bar, Amit, Bil, Peter, Yoram, and The American Friends of Unit 669, who are always on call for any mission and request of the unit's commanders and soldiers;

Eli, Suzie, Janet and Joel, thanks to you I had the chance to discover the power of vulnerability, out there in the mountains and nature, you continue to spread goodness in the world every single day;

Morris, you gave me the conviction and confidence to bring the story of Unit 669 to America—such a massive injection of encouragement that it ended up leading to the birth of another book entirely;

Arturo, Caren and Mark, you look after the members of 669 with love and care like they're your own kids;

David, Adam, and Aleigha, the stars behind the scenes, for your outstanding professionalism and profound trust;

Daniel, Caroline, and Hannah, who are working for the future of the Jewish people day and night, their faith in the way forward is constant. You taught me a great lesson in planting trees for the years to come;

Mark, Richie, Kathy, and Garry, the dedicated commando squad, with immense compassion, carrying out around-the-clock operations to make the world a better place in countless ways;

Yael and Alex, for all of your support along the way and your profound friendship—even if Noga knew you first, you're now like family to us;

Oded and Romina, it's incredible how the friendship of two army guys freezing in the Mediterranean ocean together led to such amazing things;

Joey and Stacy, for your unshakeable faith and unconditional support in embarking on this project with full steam ahead;

Max, for your remarkable modesty, enormous dreams, and your passion for saving lives and helping those in need;

Amos, my inimitable Tel Avivian grandpa, who we somehow all got lucky enough to have in our lives;

Jacob and Joe, your talents are clear on every page and in every line of this book—I couldn't have done it without you;

The Naomi Foundation, and especially **Maya and Lindsey**—you help us proliferate excellence among the next generation of Israeli physicians, so we can complete our task, which isn't just to reach the casualties, but to bring them to the best doctors and medical care in the world;

Eden, Ari, and Sivan, for the deep bond that we've all shared over the years. I know it's not easy to read about everything we've gone through;

My beloved **Nana and Nunu**, you continue to teach me how to live with joy, how to overcome hardships, the value of laughter and smiles, and the great importance of family;

Mitchell and Susan, you play such a central role in our life even though you're half a world away;

Doda Ellen, my mom's sister from Boston—you should know that I still have the legendary blanket;

And finally, **Noga—my Noga**. When you're by my side, the world is a more beautiful place. I love you more than words can express.

ABOUT THE AUTHOR

Credit: Eli Atias

Guy was born on a kibbutz in northern Israel and is a fourth-generation descendant of Israel's founding pioneers. While studying medicine at Tel Aviv University, he lectured in IDF commander courses, headed a department at a global medical research institute, and contributed to major Israeli newspapers. He also founded JIMS, a center for leadership in medical education, and has led humanitarian missions in Central America and Africa. Guy currently resides in Tel Aviv with his wife, Noga. This is his second bestselling book.